Thoughts to Ponder

Daring Observations About the Jewish Tradition

Thoughts to Ponder
Daring Observations About the Jewish Tradition

NATHAN LOPES CARDOZO

URIM PUBLICATIONS

New York • Jerusalem

To my dear wife
Frijda Rachel Lopes Cardozo
without whom life would not be possible.

҈

In memory of the unforgettable
HeChover R. Jechiel Philipson *z"l*
and his dear wife
Eva Philipson Colthof *z"l*

who served the Jewish Community in the Netherlands for nearly half a
century and the *kehilla* of Haarlem in particular for thirty years.

҈

and loving parents of our dear friends,
Eliahoe and Hadassa Philipson
Menachem and Esther Armon Philipson
Benjamin and Grace Philipson

Thoughts to Ponder: Daring Observations About the Jewish Tradition
by Nathan Lopes Cardozo
Copyright © 2002 by Nathan Lopes Cardozo

ISBN 965-7108-40-3

Urim Publications, P.O. Box 52287, Jerusalem 91521 Israel

Lambda Publishers Inc.
3709 13ᵗʰ Avenue Brooklyn, New York 11218 U.S.A.
Tel: 718-972-5449 Fax: 718-972-6307
Email: mh@ejudaica.com

www.UrimPublications.com

Designed by Raphaël Freeman
Typeset in Garamond by Jerusalem Typesetting

Contents

In memory of
our grandparents
Yamin Zion ben Yosef Nissim *z"l*
and
Farha bat Shaul Shemtob *z"l*

The Yamin-Joseph family

⟡

In memory of
my mother
Clara Haya bat Hana bat Eliezer
Schwartz Mayer,
whose truthfulness and love of justice
were admirable.

Tania Guetta

⟡

In honor of Iris Nenner,
mother of Sloimi Yehudi

Charles Nenner

⟡

With thanks to my father Cornelis
and my mother Rosalia
for the life they granted me
and thanks to
Rabbi Menachem Mendel Schneerson *z"l*
and his wife
Rebbetzin Chaya Mushka *z"l*
for bringing Judaism into my life.

Henriette Van Driel

Introduction

IT IS WITH GREAT EXCITEMENT that I offer this collection of *Thoughts to Ponder* to the public. Each "thought" is a short, and often unusual, insight into Judaism and the complexities of human existence and religious meaning. The thoughts are drawn from a collection of e-mails that were sent on a weekly basis to nearly 25,000 people. The enthusiastic reception that I received from them gave me the impetus to slightly organize these thoughts, and present them in book form.

As is true of my earlier books, some of the observations made may not be to everyone's liking. No apology is offered.

I do not claim to be original in my writing, since it is difficult to know if we really are the first to give birth to a new idea. This is even more true when one is dealing with the Jewish Tradition with its plethora of ideas. One may think that one's thoughts are original, while in truth, one's subconscious has conjured up earlier observations of others, which have been tucked away in the recesses of one's brain.

Since many of the "thoughts" relate to our holy Torah, I have included a reference index on "*Parashat Hashavua*" and the Jewish Holidays at the back of the book.

I thank Jeanne Arenstein, and Sorelle Wachmann of Urim Publications, for their superb editing, and my publisher, Tzvi Mauer, for once again taking the risk of publishing some of my thoughts.

This book is dedicated to my dear wife Frijda Rachel who has been my life companion for more than 30 years. Together we have weathered the many storms and illnesses which have befallen us. These, however, were only small disturbances compared to the immense blessings which we have been granted, including, above all, the "*nachat*" we derive from our children, children-in-law and grandchildren. Our mothers, Bertha Lopes Cardozo, Rosa Gnesin, my brother Jacques and his family, and our dear friends, Aaron and Bep Spijer and Rabbi Abraham and Irma Lopes Cardozo, were once more a source of great inspiration.

It is necessary to thank many people for making this volume possible. I refer the reader to all those mentioned in the dedication pages.

Finally, I offer my thanks to the Almighty who has given me the opportunity to write another book about His remarkable Word and world.

Nathan Lopes Cardozo
Jerusalem
Adar 5762, February 2002

1. Education and Leadership

– I –

Jewish Identity,
Jewish Leadership and Rebellion

LEADERSHIP IS ONE of the most difficult qualities for humans to attain. It requires a rare combination of wisdom, courage, knowledge and experience. Very few people possess such qualities, and even fewer know the art of combining them in a balanced way.

When looking at the astonishing story of Moshe *Rabbeinu's* rise to leadership, we are confronted with an extraordinary account of how he became fit—in what must be seen as the most challenging leadership role in Man's history—to liberate a few million slaves from an anti-Semitic dictatorship. Faced with the formidable task of teaching all of mankind the highest level of ethics, Moshe transformed the people of Israel into a nation of God.

We might think that in order to be able to inspire a few million people to fear God, one would have to receive the best religious education available, and that only the finest teachers would do. Exemplary behavior would need to be displayed, and, no doubt, would require a well-protected environment in which outside heretical ideologies could not penetrate, and in which secularity would play no role. Only under such conditions could one develop into the man who would one day be great enough to have an open encounter with God and receive His teachings. But surprisingly, in reading the story of Moshe's education, we are confronted with a different reality.

When Moshe leaves the palace of Pharaoh for the first time to visit his own enslaved brothers, he is confronted with the harsh realities of life. Right in front of him, an Egyptian strikes a Hebrew, possibly with the intention of killing him. Without hesitating, Moshe approaches the Egyptian, smites him and buries him in the ground (*Shemot* 2:12).

Bearing in mind that Moshe has just left the home of Pharaoh, in which he was raised for many years, we might wonder what was going through Moshe's mind at this moment. Whose side was he going to take? Raised in the world of Egyptian culture, receiving instruction from the elite of Egyptian educators, possibly even private tutelage from Pharaoh himself—in preparing him for the monarchy of Egypt in years to come—Moshe must have seen the Egyptian as a compatriot. This was a man of his own culture! Why take any action against him? No doubt the Hebrew must have been in the wrong and the Egyptian was justified in punishing him!

However, it seems that Moshe did have warm feelings towards the Jews, in spite of the fact that, as such, they were total foreigners to him. After all, "he came to see *his brothers*," which indicates that he was well aware of the fact that he was of Jewish stock. Psychologists would no doubt raise the question as to whether or not Moshe was plagued by an identity crisis. Did he see himself as an Egyptian or a Hebrew? How would he be able to decide on whose side he was?

A deeper reading of the verses seems to allude to this problem, and demonstrates how Moshe dealt with it.

> And he [Moshe] turned this way and that way, and he saw there was no man, and he smote the Egyptian and hid him in the sand.
>
> (*Shemot* 2:12)

As was suggested by an unknown commentator, the above verse may be alluding, albeit in an allegorical way, to the condition of Moshe's mind: *Moshe suddenly realized that he lived in two worlds.* While his youth was spent in the world of all that Egypt had to offer—as far as culture, knowledge, art and religion were concerned—his heart was somewhere else. Deep down, a Jewish voice was speaking to him, making demands upon him that opposed all of the values of Egyptian culture. It is for this reason that "*he looked this way and that way.*" He realized that he was standing at a crossroads in his life, and became aware that "*there was no man,*" i.e., that as long as he remained unsure as to which world he belonged, he was not a man of any character or strength. Faced with this dilemma, he was forced to make a decision, and consequently "*smote the Egyptian*" man *within himself* and "buried him in the sand."

This spur of the moment decision is possibly the most radical one ever to be made in human history. After all, it was *this* resolution which induced Moshe to enter into the world of Judaism and become its greatest leader, teaching mankind, Jews and gentiles, to place God at the center of their lives.

However, Moshe must have realized that by putting an end to his ambivalent situation, he would be destroying all of his future in Egypt. He would be relinquishing the opportunity of becoming the new monarch—an act that would surely turn the whole of Egypt against him—and would no doubt become instead a wanderer and refugee.

Only after this heroic act does God reveal Himself to Moshe at the Burning Bush. It appears that it is a result of this deed that God decides to make Moshe into the greatest leader of all time. Had Moshe been educated in a warm Jewish environment with the best Jewish educators to guide him, and had he been protected from the influences of the outside world, he would *not* have been able to become what he was.

It *had* to be a man who was raised in a foreign environment, committed to the idolization of a human being, and in which morality played no role, out of which the most outstanding leader of God's nation could emerge. To become a leader one must be a fighter, and no such fight takes place without an inner spiritual war. It was the "rebel within" which transformed Moshe into the leader of a nation whose function it is to be a "light unto the nations."

True, this does not mean that one should expose one's children to anti-religious philosophies, or immoral practices, so as to make them into strong Jews. Most people do not possess the immense spiritual strength of Moshe, with the capacity of utilizing secular external influences as catalysts to create spiritual power. This is only true for the very few. But it definitely means that real greatness is accomplished through boldness and the capacity to fight. Moreover, it should make Jewish educators wonder if the Jewish education they offer their students will provide them with sufficient ammunition to counter the secular world once they leave their educational institutions.

— 2 —

Weariness and Gentile Advice

Rabbi samson raphael hirsch, one of the great Jewish leaders and thinkers of modern times, draws our attention to a strange incident that occurred in the days of Moshe. After Moshe left Egypt with the great multitude of people, his father-in-law, Yitro, criticized him for the way he was administrating the Israelites.

> What is this that you are doing to the people? Why do you sit alone and all the people stand around you from morning until evening? And Moshe responded to his father-in-law: "It is because the people come to me to inquire of God. When they are solicitous about any matter, they come before me, and I decide between one person and another, and I make known the laws and the teachings of God." But Moshe's father-in-law said to him: "What you are doing is not right, you will surely wear yourself out and these people as well."
>
> (*Shemot* 18:13–21)

Yitro consequently advised Moshe to reform the existing system so that only the major problems would be brought to his personal attention, while minor issues would be decided on by a large number of wise elders who would assist him:

> You will make it easier for yourself, and they will share the burden. And Moshe heeded his father-in-law and did just as he said.
>
> (*Shemot* 18:23)

Rabbi Hirsch poses a very simple question: Could Moshe not have determined this himself? Did he not realize that he was exhausting himself and that it would just be a matter of time until he would no longer be able to cope with the situation? One does not have to be a genius to identify the problem. Besides this, Yitro's suggestion is basically a simple one. It does not require great juridical knowledge. So why did Moshe, the wisest of men, not think of this himself?

Before delving into Rabbi Hirsch's response, another question presents itself: At the end of Moshe's life, we are informed that "His eyesight was not diminished and his vigor had not abated" (*Devarim* 34:7). His physical strength exceeded the average, and, indeed, we do not see that Moshe ever got tired (except in the case where his hands became heavy when the Jews fought the Amalekites [*Shemot* 17:12]). As such, it is strange that Yitro was concerned that Moshe would suddenly feel tired while judging the people. It would not have been surprising if Moshe would have responded in the following way: "Do not worry, weariness is not troubling me. God gave me the strength to handle all those who come to see me."

However, Moshe did not make any such observation. Instead, it is very clear from the text that he was indeed most eager to implement his father-in-law's suggestion. He was getting tired!

Our question is therefore obvious: Why did he suddenly feel weary? Is it tenable that a man who survived without food and water for forty days on top of Mount Sinai could become so easily exhausted from judging people all day long? So why did God suddenly deny him his usual strength?

When contemplating this further, we could suggest that there were very good reasons for God to ensure that Moshe preserved his strength. As the great leader and teacher of Torah, it was crucial for Moshe to maintain contact with all of his people. In order to accomplish this, he would frequently have to meet with them personally, discuss their problems, and subsequently give them advice. Once he would no longer be able to do so, the people would become spiritually distanced from him. And, indeed, this seems to have happened once he implemented Yitro's advice! So what were God's motives in bringing on Moshe's sudden bouts of fatigue?

We may now turn to Rabbi Hirsch's response to his own question:

> Nothing is so instructive to us as this information regarding the first legal
> institution of the Jewish State, coming immediately before the chapter of

the Law-giving. So little was Moshe in himself a legislative genius, he had so little talent for organizing that he had to learn the first elements of state organization from his father-in-law. The man who tired himself out to utter exhaustion, and to whom of himself did not occur to arrange this, or some other simple solution equally beneficial to himself and his people, the man to whom it was necessary to have a Yitro to suggest this obvious device, that man could never have given a constitution and Laws out of his own head, that man was *only* and indeed just *because of this* the best and the most faithful instrument of God.

(*Shemot*, Isaac Levy trans., Judaica Press, 1971)

In other words, Moshe, with all his greatness, lacked the basic insight necessary to guarantee the proper administration of the juridical process. God denied him this insight in order to prove to later generations that he could never have been a lawgiver, and that the laws of Torah were not the result of his superior mind.

We would, however, like to suggest a second reason, which at the same time answers our own question. *God denied Moshe his usual strength so as to allow a non-Jew to come forward and give him advice!* The Kabbalist Rabbi Chayim Ibn Attar, known as *Ohr HaChayim*, indeed alludes to this when he writes that the very purpose of God causing Yitro to come and visit the camp of the Israelites was to teach the Jewish people that although the Torah is the all-encompassing repository of wisdom, the gentiles (although not obligated to observe all of its laws) are fundamental to its success and application. There are areas in which Jews do not excel, and where non-Jews are far more gifted. One area seems to be the skill of proper bureaucratic administration.

Judaism was, and is, never afraid to admit that the gentile world possesses much wisdom and insight. While Jews have to be a nation apart, this does not preclude them from looking beyond their own borders, and benefiting from the wisdom of outsiders.

The gentile world may not possess Torah, but it definitely *does* possess wisdom.

(*Eicha Rabati* 2:17)

It is this message which God sent to His people only a short while after He had saved them from the hands of the Egyptians. Due to their bitter experience in the land of their slavery, they had developed such animosity for anything of gentile origin that they became wholly convinced that mankind at large was anti-Semitic. God immediately crushed that thought, and sent them a righteous gentile by the name of Yitro to impress upon them that the non-Jewish world includes remarkable people who not only possess much wisdom, but who actually love the people of Israel, and contribute to Jewish life.

Viewed in this light, Moshe's sudden weariness is no mere coincidence, and comes to teach an important lesson. A Jew may start to believe that he is self-sufficient and that he can do it all alone. This attitude, rooted in his conviction that all gentiles are anti-Semitic and are therefore unreliable, could not only lead to total isolation, but also to a kind of Jewish haughtiness which is contrary to God's Will. By causing Moshe to become exhausted, God made sure that Moshe would indeed need the advice of another person.

By making Yitro into the father-in-law of the most holy Jew of all time, God made it abundantly clear that He would not tolerate any racism; even a righteous gentile can climb up to the highest ranks of saintliness. Only after that message was driven home were the Jews ready to enter the land and begin their own life as an independent nation.

− 3 −

Tolerance and Personal Conscience

In our days, the word "tolerance" has become an increasingly popular word, along with other such terms as "pluralism" and "democracy." These words are by now so frequently used that one would hope that most people have a proper understanding of their meanings. This is, however, far from true. In fact, it seems that the more these words appear in our papers, books, or conversations, the less they seem to be comprehended. Often they are used in ways that oppose the very values they stand for.

When we focus, for example, on the aforementioned word, tolerance, we are able to gain greater insight into this matter. People are often proud to show how "tolerant" they are. This means that they see themselves as very broad-minded people who really have little objection when others disagree with their own opinion. All views, attitudes and outlooks on life should be permitted in a free and democratic society.

The shallowness of such an attitude is, however, obvious. Would society indeed be prepared to be tolerant on all fronts, all hell would break loose, and it would prove to be a self-destructive measure. Little effort is needed to explain that we would not be able to be tolerant in the face of anti-Semitism, racism, public nudity, crime or sexual harassment of women and children.

Suddenly we realize that there are moral principles that cannot be violated, and, we should stand by these principles, come what may. Most people become confused when speaking about tolerance. They often use this word when, in fact, they speak out of apathy.

Alexander Chase once wrote:

The peak of tolerance is most readily achieved by those who are not burdened by any convictions.

(Perspectives, 1966)

Ogden Nash expressed it in the following way:

> Sometimes with secret pride, I sigh
> How tolerant am I,
> Then wonder what is really mine,
> Tolerance or a rubber spine.

Indeed, most of the time it is indifference that makes people believe that they are tolerant. It is easy to be tolerant when one does not care about values and principles or about the moral needs of society and one's fellow individual.

As the saying goes: *If one does not stand for anything, one will fall for everything.* Tolerance has become the hiding place for many people to turn their egocentricity into a virtue.

When focusing on the Jewish scene of today, we see a similar phenomenon. This time it is "unity" which has become a popular word used by the various sections of the Jewish world. All of them speak of unity, and each one accuses the others of a lack of commitment towards that goal.

No one would argue that the unity of the Jewish people is not of crucial importance. If the Jewish people would fragment into several sections in such a way that unity could no longer be maintained, we would indeed face a most serious problem that could quite well be detrimental to the future of the People of Israel. Still, we have to ask ourselves if unity is really an ultimate goal to strive for as the highest value.

To many people, the refusal by a major part of the Orthodox leadership to recognize the Conservative and Reform movements as legitimate representatives of Judaism is a sign of weakness, and a lack of both courage and tolerance. While it is fully understandable why many are disturbed by this attitude, it would be entirely wrong to attribute this to weakness and lack of courage on the side of the Orthodox.

There is obviously a great deal to say in favor of cooperation and mutual recognition between all these movements. Indeed, to be able to agree to a kind of compromise is a sign of strength and flexibility. In addition, one could argue that the refusal by the Orthodox to bend causes a great amount of irreparable damage. There are no overtures to reconciliation, there is no attempt at mutual understanding; instead, accusations fly on an emotional level, and all attempts to find a solution are completely undermined.

One could even argue that through some form of compromise, the image that Orthodox Judaism presents to the outside world would be more positive, identified less as an extreme religious movement, and would be more palatable to the non- and even anti-Orthodox members of Jewry. Some earlier opponents would perhaps join its ranks.

There is, however, one "but." All the above would be true if religion would belong to that category which also includes matters such as politics, economics and science. But it does not. However important unity may be, when speaking about religious matters, unity, as such, is not the priority. What is the priority is *personal conscience.*

Let us for a moment examine the history of Judaism. Should Avraham have made a compromise with the world in which he lived for the purpose of unity? Wouldn't this strong-minded man have been more influential if he would not have taken the stand he did? Clearly, Avraham created much emotional upheaval. He and so many prophets after him, like Shmuel, Yeshayahu and Yirmiyahu, were impassioned protestors who refused to go along with the values of their days. No doubt, many saw them as extremists and inflexible leaders who shattered the tranquility of their societies. More than that, we can be sure that many "modern-minded" men in those days condemned them for their outdated ideologies and refusal to conform with "modern" values. It may be worthwhile for us to consider a major controversy that plagued the Christian world for a long time. One of the most famous Anglican theologians in the nineteenth century was John Henry Newman. After holding a foremost position in the Anglican Church, he decided to defect to the Catholic Church, and later became one of its most prominent cardinals. At the time, this move became a topic of intensive debate throughout the Christian world.

Many of Newman's admirers believed that he should have stayed in the Anglican Church. They correctly believed that from the point of view of reconciliation, he would have been able to make a major contribution towards religious tolerance. He would have been considered as a most authoritative

Anglican with a strong tendency to Rome. The Anglican Church would not have been able to ignore him in such a position, and he would have been able to bring both positions closer together, on the road to reconciliation. But the moment he became a Catholic, the Anglican Church wrote him off.

When asked why indeed he had not taken that route and stayed in the Anglican Church, Newman made a most important observation. After admitting that he would indeed have been much more influential had he stayed in the Anglican Church, and, as such, would have contributed to a much needed reconciliation, he added that this option was not open to him. His words are most telling: *One cannot put reconciliation before one's conscience.* In matters of truth, one makes a choice between what one considers to be true and what one considers to be false. Newman had come to the conclusion that the theology of the Anglican Church was erroneous and had to be rejected. To stay in the Anglican Church would have been a compromise, and as such, a sign of weakness and lack of courage.

This historic event should be of major importance for Jews when debating the question of the authenticity of the Reform and Conservative movements. Neither Jewish identity nor the nature of Judaism can be determined simply on the basis of what will be less detrimental to Jewish unity. This is an instance where personal conscience, i.e., one's perception of the truth, is an overriding consideration.

For Orthodox Judaism, the Torah and Oral Tradition are deeply rooted in the Sinaitic experience. The Torah is seen as a verbal revelation of God's Will, and no human being is able to reject anything stated there. Likewise, the Oral Torah is the officially accepted interpretation of the Torah text as understood in classical Jewish sources, and, while open to some debate, should not be even partially rejected or ignored. Obviously, anybody has the right to challenge this belief and reject it. But nobody could impugn the Orthodox for standing its ground by refusing to compromise on these fundamental beliefs. To Orthodox Jews, this is a matter of truth or falsehood. The Conservative and Reform movements have rejected their beliefs in their own way and in varying degrees. That the Orthodox therefore do not want to recognize the Reform and Conservative views as being representative of authentic Judaism is not the outcome of weakness, but of principle. It is a matter of personal conscience where no compromise is possible.

Cardinal Newman would have understood.

– 4 –
Tolerance and Dialogue

In the last chapter, we argued that personal conscience is of prime value and that one should not confuse tolerance with apathy. For this reason, Orthodoxy's refusal to compromise on its own principles, so as to appease the Reform and Conservative movements, should only be honored and respected. Even unity cannot always be the final arbiter.

This does not mean, however, that dialogue cannot take place between Orthodoxy and these movements. Objections may be raised that such dialogues could be (and have been) unsuccessful since the parties involved have too many ideological differences, therefore making any reconciliation utterly impossible. This may very well be true, but it is not only the desire to find an ideological *solution* that makes a dialogue meaningful. There are several other important dimensions that should be carefully considered.

First of all, there is the purely psychological dimension. When two people bitterly disagree, much animosity could be prevented by just making sure that they meet. Human experience shows that as long as two people do not physically meet, look each other in the eye, and see each other smile, they often develop completely mistaken impressions of their opponents. In that case, an important component for proper dialogue is missing. One should, after all, never forget that the success of a dialogue is not only dependent upon the strength of the speaker's argument, but also on the purely physiological impressions that they convey: such as a smile, a laugh, or even the way one sits, how one looks at the opponent, and how one lifts one's eyebrows.

It may even be the case that both parties will come closer through dialogue, and start to understand why the other happens to stand for a very different point of view. On a significant number of occasions, Orthodoxy was able not only to explain its positions to the other parties, but actually succeeded in making the others at least *respect* its point of view.

It is most important to remember that all forms of pietistic obscurantism ultimately lead to one's own defeat. We would do well to remember the wise words of the Maharal of Prague who was perhaps the greatest thinker and defender of authentic Judaism of his day, and whose words are, until this very day, studied by many who believe in Orthodox Judaism. After quoting Averroes, one of the greatest Islamic philosophers and Aristotelian commentators, he writes:

> ...It is proper, out of love of reason and knowledge, that you not [summarily] reject anything that opposes your own ideas, especially so if [your adversary] does not intend merely to provoke you, but rather to declare his beliefs.... When our *Rishonim* [the earlier Jewish sages up till the fifteenth century] found something written against their faith, they did not reject it [out of hand], for it stands to reason that [such opposition] ought not to be a cause for rejecting it and silencing a man when it comes to religious matters; for religion is given to all. This is especially so with regard to the written word... should there not have been a reaction against the books of the philosophers who, following their own investigations, repudiated [traditional religious teachings] and asserted the eternity of the universe and thus denied the creation altogether? Nevertheless [the *Rishonim*] read their books and did not dismiss them. For the proper way to attain the truth is to hear [others'] arguments which they sincerely hold, not out of a desire to provoke you. Thus, it is wrong simply to reject an opponent's ideas; instead, draw him close to you and delve into his words....
>
> (*"Be'er HaGolah"*, end of last chapter, translated by Dr. Norman Lamm,
> *Torah Ummada*, Jason Aronson, pp. 57–58)

These words are in no way a concession, but are a "heroic assertion of self-confidence in his faith as a believing Jew, one ready to meet all challenges...." (Lamm, ibid). It is important to remember that religious Jews have nothing to lose when confronting the truth, and it may quite well be beneficial to hear the views of those who oppose traditional Judaism. It could only be constructive to rethink and to reformulate the traditional positions so as to make them clearer and intellectually sophisticated. For as Logan Pearsall

Smith once remarked, "For souls in growth, great quarrels are great emancipations" (Afterthoughts, 1993, p. 1).

It is no doubt true that not everybody is able to confront heretical views and defeat them as the Maharal was able to do, but it would be a major mistake to believe that all dialogue should therefore be condemned. Only when the opponent is motivated by spiteful polemics should one refuse to enter into any discussion.

– 5 –

Alan M. Dershowitz, *Klotz Kashes* and The *Chozrim Beshe'ela* Movement

Lately, the state of israel is experiencing a new phenomenon. As is well known, the "*Ba'al Teshuva* movement," which includes thousands of secular Jews who have returned to Judaism, has made a major impact on Israeli society. Many young people, who were once immersed in extreme secularity, are feeling the need to reconnect with their own heritage and are finding their way back to Torah and Tradition. This new reality has given rise to the establishment of many highly successful institutions such as Aish HaTorah, Ohr Somayach, Machon Meir and Nevei Yerushalayim.

Recent information from the Israeli media suggests that a different movement is on its way. This time, it is called the movement of *Chozrim Beshe'ela*, literally "Those Who Return to Questioning," which includes many religious youth who have decided to abandon Judaism and its practices. Many of them have thrown off their *kippot* and exchanged their skirts for tight pants or even "minis," and have adopted new secular lifestyles.

Radio interviews were recently conducted in which journalists invited spoke to several of these young people, and those who assist them in integrating into the secular community. In these interviews, several disturbing facts rose to the surface which demand careful attention from the religious community, and primarily its leaders and educators.

It became clear that most of those who were interviewed did not qualify at all for such a commendable title as "Those Who Returned to Questioning."

The reason is clear. When asked about their motivations for abandoning their Judaism, almost none of those interviewed were able to express themselves in an intellectual way. Not one expressed sincere objections towards the Jewish Tradition. In fact, it became evident that no real and profound questions concerning the Jewish Tradition really perturbed them. Most responses were of an emotional nature, and often did not consist of more than statements like "I wanted to be free," "I like to dance with boys," or, even, "I do not really know." (For several interviews, see also: "*Noar Hakipot Hazerukot,*" Dr. Shraga Fisherman, Orot Yisrael, School of Education, 1998, [Hebrew].)

This does not mean that one should dismiss the emotional responses of the interviewees. No doubt, one should look beyond their seeming veneer of an emotionally driven reaction, and heed their cry for help or their inner yearning for inspiration, which may be sorely lacking in their lives. Religious educators devote little attention to this fact. Would they do so, many of these problems could be avoided.

What was also remarkable about the interviews was the conspicuous absence of those who had decided to join the Conservative or Reform movements after concluding that the Orthodox approach was wanting. All opted for an extreme, secular lifestyle in which the pleasure motive reigned high.

Even more telling was the fact that the interviewers did not even bother to ask their interviewees if they had actually studied the Jewish Tradition in great length, or if they had ever read any critiques on Judaism. Questions such as "Were those critiques the ones which made you realize that you should abandon the Jewish Tradition?" were not asked. It seemed that the interviewers were well aware of the poor intellectual quality of these young people, and were, above all, afraid that this matter would come to the surface.

It speaks volumes that those who help these young people (such as psychologists and teachers) to integrate into a secular lifestyle never seem to ask the youth if they really abandoned the Jewish Tradition for any intelligent or rational reasons. Equally disturbing is the fact that most of these professionals never bothered to consult an open-minded religious teacher, thinker or rabbi or ask such educators to speak to them at cultural evenings or meetings.

All in all, one is forced to conclude that the absence of intellectual reasoning from these young people reflects badly on the Israeli and Jewish society at large. Instead of seeing people leaving the fold because they are bothered with serious questions concerning the Jewish Tradition, we find a majority leaving for the wrong reasons: *It is not for the lack of answers that they leave but for the absence of questions!* (That is not to say, however, that all those who turned to Judaism did so with the correct motives either!)

This, however, should not lead us to believe that there *are* no good questions, and that likewise there are no young people—sincere questioners—who felt the need to leave the fold. Not every case of defection can be seen as the result of intellectual apathy.

Alan M. Dershowitz, the famous author of *Chutzpa* and *The Vanishing American Jew*, complains in his latest book, *The Genesis of Justice*, about his teachers in Yeshiva who often told him that he asked "*klotz kashes*," i.e., questions which were considered to be foolish, and as a result, should not be bothered with. The truth, however, is that most of these questions, as he repeats them in his book, are, in fact, profound, requiring a sincere response. These are not the traditional talmudic questions, but those which related to Jewish belief and Weltanschauung. Quite clearly, the teachers did not know the answers themselves and therefore consigned them to the "*klotz kashes*" category.

This is a major tragedy which has led to the loss from Orthodox Judaism of many sincere probing Jewish minds throughout the world. There are no *klotz kashes*, and even if there are, they should not be treated as such. A good teacher must develop the art of taking any real *klotz kashe* and restating it in such a way that it becomes profound, so as not to embarrass the student. Above all, the teacher must not make the student feel that he/she is trying "to get out" of answering the question.

Schools, *yeshivot* and their teachers should allocate plenty of time for questions from their students. No student should ever feel that questions are not to be asked or are not welcome. The commonly repeated response by teachers: "God said so. You'd better believe it, case closed" is a deathblow to many competent students, who otherwise would have continued with their Jewish studies, attempting to find many of the answers on their own.

It is true that not all questions can be answered on the spot, and teachers definitely have the right to ask their students to have some patience so that they can supply the answer at a later time. But they should never give the student the feeling that they are trying to get out of it. It is far better to admit, "I really do not know," than to be silent and hope that the student will forget. He won't.

Conversely, students should also learn that not every question can always be answered to their satisfaction, as some people may like to believe.

Sometimes, the best answer is to concede that the question remains. But students should be taught *why* that is the case and that such questions are just as common, if not more so, in secular philosophies.

It was Frank Moore Colby who once observed: "Clever people seem to feel the natural pleasure of bewilderment and are always answering questions when the chief relish of life is to go on asking them" (*Simple Simon: The Colby Essays*, vol. 1, 1926). Or as the Yiddish equivalent goes: "*Man starbt nicht von a kashe*" (One does not die from a question).

One is indeed reminded of John Fowles' famous observation, "An answer is always a form of death" (The Magus, 1965, p. 75).

Still, the Orthodox world should realize that the *Chozrim Beshe'ela* movement is not so much a product of secular philosophies, but of the Orthodox educational system. If Orthodox teachers were prepared to acknowledge and encourage questioning in their classrooms, it would give rise to the kind of *Chozrim Beshe'ela* who are asking probing questions with all sincerity. Instead of becoming frustrated and alienated, these people would start realizing the profundity of Judaism.

– 6 –

Educating Towards Enjoyment

Rₐʙʙɪ ᴍᴇɪʀ sɪᴍᴄʜᴀ ᴏғ ᴅᴠɪɴsᴋ, author of *Meshech Chochma*, draws our attention to one of the most powerful messages Jewish education has to offer. When discussing the sin of Adam and Chava—that they did not abstain from the Tree of Knowledge—this commentary draws our attention to one of the most common mistakes made in Jewish education.

Why did Adam and Chava eat from the tree? Did the Garden of Eden not include many trees with the most appealing fruits and delicious tastes that were permitted? Why would primordial Man become obsessed with *one* forbidden tree when all other trees are permissible? Our sages and many psychologists would no doubt respond that this is due to the fact that human nature is more tempted by the forbidden than it is by the permitted: "Stolen waters are sweet" is a well-known saying. It is not that water, as such, is sweet, just that it becomes sweet once it is stolen.

Does this imply, therefore, that resisting the forbidden is beyond the capacity of most human beings? In that case, God's commandment not to eat from the tree would become a trial that no human could pass. As such, this prohibition would be morally unjustifiable.

When one looks into the text, it seems that God's *first* commandment to Adam was an uncompromising *prohibition* against eating from the Tree of Knowledge. This would mean that Man's first encounter with the Will of God was of a negative nature: a restriction. But, maintains *Meshech Chochma*, this is far from true: careful analysis of the text shows quite a different story.

"And God the Lord commanded man as follows: From all the trees in the garden *'achol tochel'* (*Bereishit* 2:16)." This Hebrew expression (using a double expression for "eating") does not mean, "You are permitted to eat," but "You *shall* eat!" In other words, God's first communication with Man was not relayed in the negative, but was a positive commandment to "eat and be merry."

Adam's negative psychological makeup, however, caused him to misunderstand this communication. Instead of seeing his encounter with God in a positive light, he started his religious life on the wrong foot in the belief that religion *must* start with the negative. This, however, is far from the truth. The story of the Tree of Knowledge teaches a person that the only way in which one can deal with prohibitions and restrictions is when they are preceded by positive demands. Since religious life starts on a positive note, and God's first commandment to Man is to enjoy His creation, a person's perspective, even of the forbidden, is one of promise. His attitude towards the restrictions is influenced and is imbued with optimism.

Without any doubt, this has become one of the gravest stumbling blocks of religious education. When Judaism is introduced to a person as a religion of taboos, permanent damage is inflicted upon its very structure. Too often, young people have become victims of such negativity and consequently have not been able to find their way to the Jewish experience. One of the greatest tasks of Jewish educators today is to daringly turn the tide and show our people that Judaism is foremost the art of enjoying God's world.

Once it becomes clear that God started His conversation with Man on a positive note, all the prohibitions fall into place. The goal of Judaism's restrictions is not to form a tradition of prohibitions with the purpose of making life more difficult. A closer study of those restrictions will show that their main purpose is to give life a higher meaning. And this meaning will never become apparent unless it is shaped by discipline. Life, after all, is an art, and art is an emotion *controlled* by an idea.

The bottom line is this: if one does not first teach oneself to enjoy God's creation, one will end up transgressing His laws.

When Times Change,
Methods for Jewish Education Change

As HAS BEEN CONSTANTLY stressed by our sages, the contents of the Torah are not subject to change so as to make it appear more progressive. While progress is, no doubt, a matter of great value without which society cannot function, one is reminded of G. K. Chesterton's famous observation that many people believe that progress is "leaving things *behind* us, which has utterly obscured the real idea of growth, which means leaving things *inside* us" (*The Romance of Rhyme: Fancies versus Fads*, 1923).

"It is not the Torah which needs to change to the spirit of modern times, but it is modern times which have to accommodate themselves to the spirit of the Torah" (Rabbi Samson Raphael Hirsch). While such an observation is much more complex than many believe it to be, it is definitely true that throughout history, since the time of *Moshe Rabbeinu* till our own days, there has never been controversy over how a) *tefillin* need to be updated, b) *mezuzot* need to be upgraded, or c) how *tzitzit* need to look more progressive. While theoretical disputes appear in the Talmud concerning some of these issues, the practical *Halacha* has always remained the same. This can be said about most halakhic cases, although not all of them.*

There is one outstanding and definitive exception to this rule of the constancy of *Halacha*, and that is Jewish education. The Talmud in *Baba Batra* (21a) informs us: "First, if a child had a father, his father taught him [Torah],

---

* See my *Judaism on Trial*, Urim Publications (Jerusalem, 2000) p. 57.

and if he had no father, he did not learn at all." This was based on the verse, "And you shall teach your sons...." (*Devarim* 11:19). Later on, the prophets or sages "made an ordinance that teachers of children should be appointed in Jerusalem," and children from the outlying areas of Israel should be brought to the Holy City. The verse to support this was "For from Tzion the Torah shall go out" (*Yeshayahu* 2:3). When this ordinance lost its effectiveness, and too many children were lacking a Jewish education, it became mandatory to have teachers stationed in all towns and provinces. Once it became clear that this too would be ineffective, and many young children under the age of 16 would still not receive any elementary instruction, "Rabbi Yehoshua ben Gamla came and ordained that teachers of young children should be appointed in each district and town, and that children should enter school at age six or seven...." (*Baba Batra* 21a).

This talmudic observation holds great meaning. While sages considered "new rulings" as illegitimate, even "when times may have asked for it," such opinions were absolutely rejected when it came to the question of *how* to instruct Jewish children. Nowhere do we see more innovative strategies in Judaism than in the area of Jewish education. As times changed, the methods for teaching Judaism changed. Although the Talmud does not discuss the actual syllabus, it is clear that it had this in mind when it made the above observations. (See the published essay on Jewish education by Rabbi Yaakov Kamenetsky *z"l*, which deals with the question of why Jewish children today are no longer taught by the method suggested in *Pirkei Avot* 5.)

Jewish education has only one goal, and that is to inspire students to reach for Heaven (*Yirat Shamayim*)—to transform them into outstanding human beings, who demonstrate concern for their fellowmen and dedication towards the Jewish people and mankind, according to the commandments of the Torah. The moment any educational system is no longer able to achieve that goal, it becomes outdated and dangerous, however much it may have succeeded in previous generations. The often repeated slogan in certain Orthodox circles, "This is the way our forefathers taught Torah in Presburg or Istanbul, so it must work today as well, and what could be wrong with it?" is of no value unless it is abundantly clear that such a system indeed works in the twenty-first century. The heavy bombardment of modern influences on society, from which even the most Orthodox cannot escape, requires constant contemplation and innovation by highly competent Jewish educators. When this new reality demands totally different approaches or drastic changes in the syllabi in schools or *yeshivot, nothing* should hold back those who are responsible from making these changes. No doubt this requires courage. "But courage is resistance to fear, mastery of fear—not absence of fear" (Mark Twain).

Part of the religious world today has fallen prey to a kind of religious behaviorism, that believes that Judaism glorifies the deed without proper motivation and inspiration. We are blessed with synagogues and educational institutions, but how many of the worshipers are still connected with "inner life?" Many religious children receive an excellent Jewish education, but to what degree are they taught the art of appreciation?

Failure to grasp this reality will ultimately lead to the vulgarization of Judaism, of which there is already much evidence today.

What a person *does* is only the minimum of what a person *is*. Deeds are outpourings; they are not the essence of the self. This does not, in any way, minimize the importance of the Jewish belief that outer deeds create inner feelings and mentalities. The heart is, after all, a lonely voice in the busy marketplace of the living. But without constantly emphasizing the fact that all observance is ultimately for the sake of transformation of the whole person, Judaism will not be a beloved friend of the child and student. This is the holy task of Jewish education which confronted sages in each generation: to consider the need to change the rules of Jewish study programs so as to accomplish the maximum.

11. Jewish Family and Society

− 8 −

Krepelach and Bissli
The Revelation of a Language

Words, in their primary or immediate signification,
stand for nothing but the ideas in the mind
of him who uses them.
(John Locke, An Essay Concerning Human
Understanding, 1690, 3.2.2)

Language is the most revelational expression of a person's inner thoughts and attitudes. Freud made us aware of this when he discussed the "slip of the tongue" phenomenon. It is in one's language that a person reveals one's inner life. The subconscious overflows and before one is aware of it, one has already exposed one's inner self.

It is the nature of languages to be constantly in flux. Whole societies and their changing attitudes can be identified by studying their use of certain words and expressions, including those which have fallen into disuse and those which have replaced them.

The Hebrew language is a most powerful example of this phenomenon. A comparison drawn between how the biblical and talmudic mind used Hebrew, and how the language has steadily deteriorated in our days, is most telling.

It has often been noted that Hebrew does not possess a word which is equivalent to the expression, "to have." Erich Fromm in his monumental book, *To Have or To Be*, commented on this:

> To those who believe that "to have" is a most natural category of human existence, it may come as a surprise to learn that many languages have no word for "to have." In Hebrew, for instance, "I have" must be expressed by the indirect form, "*yesh li*" (it is to me). In fact, languages that express possession in this way, rather than by "I have," predominate. It is interesting to note that in the development of languages the construction, "it is to me," is followed later on by the construction, "I have," but as Emile Benveniste has pointed out, the evolution does not occur in the reverse direction. (Erich Fromm, *To Have or To Be*, Abacus, London, 1979, p. 32)

This does not mean that there is no such concept as possession in Hebrew. Rather, the difference between the secular and religious attitude towards property is that the secular approach emphasizes the development of private property in which property in itself becomes dominant (even without a specific function), while the biblical attitude only knows of functional property, i.e., property, not for the sake of possession, but for use.

While modern Hebrew still does not possess a word which really expresses "to have," the language is becoming more and more "property" inclined.

Over the past few decades, we have experienced, to our great regret, a vulgarization of the Hebrew language. This is not only noticeable in Israeli society at large, but is also evident when hearing Israeli leaders and debates in the Knesset, Israel's parliament. While at the inception of the State, one would be able to enjoy a Knesset debate because of the use of superior Hebrew, today we feel increasingly uncomfortable listening to some of the members of this institution using Hebrew slang. Even some rabbinical figures who used to speak a dignified language have lowered themselves in this respect.

This new reality has entered into the collective consciousness of Israeli society. While in earlier days, the content of Israeli advertisements reflected a Jewish outlook on life, today this is often no longer the case. Years ago, when trying to convince people to buy sweets and other delicacies, names such as "krepelach," "bagelach" and "rogelach," were used. All emphasize the relationship we have with other people. These names all end with the Hebrew word "*lach*," "to you." This is not accidental. While those who created these names may not have been aware of their choice of words, their subconscious revealed inherently Jewish values.

While examining modern Hebrew advertisements we see a rather disturbing change: No longer is it "*lach*" which invites people to buy various tasty foods, but "*li*" (me): "Bissli," "Prili," "Kinli," "Egozi," "Ta'ami." One of the most recent advertisements says, "*Tehe Egoist ad haSof*" (Be an egoist until the end).

We would do well to take note of this shift in language. Like the Freudian slip of the tongue, such expressions reveal more than we would like to admit. Ultimately, it indicates how Israeli society is falling prey to Western values (or rather indicates an absence of values), in which areas such as relationship and love are seriously distorted. For many, love for others, or even for spouse and child, is nothing more than the use of another human being for one's own pleasure. The expression, "falling in love" is a case in point. Anybody who has any understanding of love knows that while one may be able to fall into a pit, one cannot "fall" in love, but only walk, stand or grow in love. It is even more important to remember that love does not exist if it is not motivated by a deep commitment to give. The Hebrew word, "*ahava*" (love), has as its root, "*hav*," which, indeed, means to give. Those who do not know the art of giving do not have the capacity to love.

Frank Leahy once observed that "Egotism is the anesthetic that dulls the pain of foolishness" (Look, January, 10, 1955). Israeli society, and the world at large, would do well to start listening once more to the language of the Torah; it could help overcome much of society's problems.

– 9 –

Boredom*

It may well be true that Man's greatest enemy today is boredom. When reading the papers, watching television or listening to the radio, we are confronted with the most absurd manifestations of dullness and apathy. There are people who spend their time rolling around Europe in a barrel, couples who dance the Charleston for more than thirty hours, and still others who have perfected the art of eating more ice cream than any human since the days of pre-historic Man, in the hope of seeing their name in print in the Guinness Book of Records.

We, as average humans, are obviously deeply impressed, and most happy to read, that at least some geniuses have arrived at the ultimate meaning of life. They have accomplished what nobody would have ever dreamed was humanly possible.

What is boredom? Boredom comes about because, in our modern world, our wishes are too easily and quickly satisfied. The pressure of fulfilling one's desires subsides, and we immediately look for new pressures, because they frame our existence. We are like deep-sea fish. We need atmospheric pressure, and without it, we are lost. Since Western Man is easily able to satisfy most of his wishes, he starts to look to absurd manifestations in order to satiate his need for pressure.

Remarkable is the fact that in the last fifty years we have transformed the most beneficial occupations into anti-boredom devices. Take the pursuit of running, which once used to be a most healthy form of exercise, until we

---

* The following two thoughts are inspired by the Dutch author Godfried J. A. Bomans.

decided to turn it into a contest in which people are forced to run harder than they are capable of doing. Some end up in hospital, others commit suicide, simply because they did not succeed in breaking the record. It has been suggested on several occasions that these people should be fined for their failure to observe the flowers on the road or the beautiful landscape while running. This was, however, abandoned on the grounds that those who won the race received the flowers in the end, and this time from the hands of a pretty young lady. Even more astonishing is the case of those swimmers who attempt to cross the channel between Calais and Dover. They seem to be unaware of the fact that there is a ferry service which would deliver them to their destination much faster.

All this would be well and good, and we could listen to a pop group of the sixties who, while discussing the problem of "*beatle zeman*" used to sing, "Let it be, let it be...." But problems arise when some thoroughly bored people start disturbing their fellow citizens in ways which would have been unimaginable some years ago. It has become commonplace that while erecting one's folding chair in a seemingly quiet place, such as a seashore or forest, with the intention of listening to the waves of the sea, or the blowing of the wind, the peace is suddenly disrupted by the blaring noise of a CD player which is turned up in full blast. Looking in the direction from where the noise is coming, we see a young man lounging in his folding chair smiling at us, as if to say, "Go ahead, make my day!"

His parents will tell you that it also disturbs them, but they are not able to do anything about it. "Youth must have its fling!" This is the well-known stopgap used whenever some youngsters are planning to do the totally unacceptable. It turns *chutzpa* into necessary therapy "required for the further development of a youngster who will otherwise not be able to become a respectable member of society." Anybody not giving him "his fling" is depriving the world of a future genius and should experience great guilt.

It is remarkable that most parents seem to believe that their children should have "their fling" so as to guarantee their proper development. This is even more surprising since these parents are the same people who fanatically cut the grass and bushes in their garden, because they know that otherwise chaos will follow. But to apply similar thoughts when they try to educate their children never occurs to them. When they read the papers about the wantonness of today's youth, they shake their heads in dismay.

Having "one's fling" *should* mean to prove oneself, as the German expression, "ausleben," conveys. It is the means to live out the potential within oneself. One particular capacity that people are endowed with is the ability to care about other human beings. One who has not maximized their potential in this way has not yet had their "fling" because one of the most beautiful aspects of being human has been withheld from them.

Our sages make a most interesting observation (*Eruvin* 65b) when they state that a man's character can be tested in three different ways: *be'kiso, be'koso, u've'ka'aso*. *By his pocket*, is he a miser or a spendthrift? *By his cup*, how does he respond to alcoholic excess? And *by his temper*, can he control himself when provoked? But, according to one of the sages, there is a fourth test which reveals a great deal about a human being's character, *af be'sahako*, also *how he plays*, i.e., how he spends his free time.

It might be frivolous to argue that the future of our society will depend on the bowling industry, but there can be no doubt that Western civilization, including the State of Israel, is slowly becoming a place where people see their fulfillment in life through the eyes of those who dance the Charleston for thirty hours. That they will get dizzy is certain, though their entry into *Olam Haba*, the world to come, is not guaranteed.

– 10 –

More on Boredom

BOREDOM IS A MULTI-FACETED phenomenon in our days and we may well be justified in considering yet another dimension of this destructive force.

In the "olden days," it was a privilege to be mature. It was something people would strive for. It meant maturity of attitude, and a great amount of experience and knowledge of how to deal with the problems of life. It also meant well-considered opinions. This is no longer the case. This is not due to the fact that younger people have become more experienced or knowledgeable, but rather because the older generation, i.e., those who used to be considered mature, have suddenly shown signs of immaturity. They have stopped being grown-up. This is evident in the way that the older generation utilizes their free time. While in earlier days, people would use their leisure time to engage in creative work for which they had no time during the working week, today we find that most "mature" people are reverting back to their childhood days. They watch television, go to a movie or spend their time in bed. This is exactly what they did when they were younger: hear, watch and sleep—passive behavior.

Passivity, indeed, is no longer the "privilege" of the young. It has become the preferred norm for all ages. As a result, the distinction between young and old has been obliterated. There is a distinct difference between a father who is involved in a creative activity, even if it is only building a hen house, and a father sitting for hours in front of a television screen. In the first case, he is mature; in the second case, he has returned to his immature days. And it is exactly through these activities that their children view their parents. The

47

parent may be a professor at a university, but at home he has regressed to his childhood. This is not to deny the value of watching television. Sometimes television offers excellent programs. But one has to realize that one is selling one's birthright for a soup of lentils.

The difference of age is revealed primarily in the way in which free time is utilized. When the behavior of adults is identical to that of youngsters, all distinction has faded. The resulting loss of dignity of the older generation in the eyes of the young is inevitable. Strangely, however, this does not mean that the mature (the parents) admit to their immaturity, but that the immature (the child) considers him/herself to be mature. The son recognizes that he does the same as his father: nothing! And it is from this unhealthy environment that the son models his life: he clothes himself with the garments of maturity which his father has rejected.

But there is another issue at stake here. Our problem also relates to the decline in religious consciousness, manifested in the disappearance of the belief in the "afterlife." In earlier days, the youth displayed a degree of respect for the elderly, because they were closer to death and therefore closer to the "truth." Somehow elderly people were "nearly there." A few more years, months or days and they would enter the "real thing." As such, the elderly person sat close to the door, while the younger ones were still in the waiting room. Today, however, this is no longer the case. The elder is no longer seen as the one who is "nearly there," but rather as one who is "nearly nowhere." This has entered into the communal consciousness of contemporary Man. The elderly man or woman have lost their grandeur, and younger contemporary generations see these senior figures as having served their turn.

All in all, parents would be well advised to reconsider their role in the eyes of their children. In their desire to show themselves to be "one of the boys" in the eyes of their children, parents run the risk of losing their dignity in their regression to juvenile behavior. Consequently, the child will no longer honor his or her parents and will not relate to them as being a source of wisdom from years of experience. Instead of seeing his or her parents climb the ladder of maturity, the child will see them descending into emptiness.

– II –

Thoughts on Dolls and Other Toys

ONE OF THE MOST unique talents which human beings are blessed with is the faculty of imagination. Unlike any other creature, human beings have a nearly unlimited potential for constructive fantasy.

In fact, our civilization is built on imagination. Without this human capacity, no progress could ever be made, whether in science, literature, philosophy, art, music or commerce. Our world would not be able to sustain itself and develop in a proper way if human beings did not continuously explore new and unutilized pathways. It is for this reason that every generation must make sure that its youngsters are provided with enough opportunities to develop a healthy imagination.

Children's toys have become a major industry. In the last few decades, we have witnessed a boom in the manufacturing of the most sophisticated toys. Today it is possible to buy dolls which can walk, sing, speak with other dolls, sleep, cry, smile, and even need diapers. No doubt, in a few more years the doll industry will confuse its clients with their evermore lifelike dolls—to the extent that their manufacturers will rush to the City Hall to register them as new births. The same can be said of electric trains, boats and planes, etc. Some of the electric cars which one can buy in toy stores can travel at a speed of 50 kilometers an hour, are equipped with radios, computers and windscreen wipers, and can operate on solar power.

While our society welcomes these new innovations in the field of entertainment—regarding them as a great benefit to our children and grandchildren—this focus is a major educational mistake.

The Torah is often referred to as a toy. King David said:

Were not Your Torah my plaything, I would have perished in my affliction.

(*Tehillim* 119:92)

This concept is found throughout many parts of Tanach. Just like playing brings joy to a human being, so does the Torah. But from what is this joy composed? No doubt, one of the many elements which contribute to the pleasure of playing is the use of the faculty of imagination. *Joy is the art of seeing great possibilities.* When people learn Torah, it is not just the information that they assimilate which is enjoyable, but, above all, they thrive on the possibility of creating new insights, "*chiddushim*," in developing one's own imagination in the pursuit of understanding the Torah. This is one of the reasons why the Oral Torah was never completely recorded and why the Torah and, later, the Talmud, were written in a most cryptic script, requiring the student to read between the lines in order to fully grasp the profundity within. It allows the mind to expand, demanding much creativity. "It is impossible that a *Beit HaMidrash* will not contain a *chiddush*" (*Chagiga* 3a). One needs to use one's own imagination to add what the text itself does not reveal.

One of the most important benefits of playing with toys is the fulfillment of children's need to *pretend*. Children do not play with the toy itself, but rather with what they *imagine* while they are playing. And the greater the distance there is between the toy and the product of the child's imagination, the more intensive and beneficial is this pursuit to the child. The child will have to use all his or her imagination to create the world in which he wants to find him/ herself.

It is for this reason that it is highly undesirable that toys should approximate reality. A doll which can speak, cry or smile is not a real doll, precisely because it is so "real." A child is not being allowed to pretend because the manufacturer has already done it for him or her. Because adults do not have the same degree of imagination as do children, they mistakenly believe they need to produce toys which look real. What they do not understand is that the children themselves will imagine the part which is missing. To be sure, the child will *initially* be very pleased with a state-of-the-art doll which can sing and smile, but a child is not aware of his or her own psychological make-up, and will ultimately soon become bored. There is, after all, very little left for the imagination. In fact, more and more parents complain that the more expensive the toy, the sooner it is likely to be neglected.

No doubt, toy manafacturers are making more money than they ever did before, but it is not serving to improve children's education. For a healthy future, we need adults who are gifted with a healthy imagination. For that we need simple educational dolls for our children.

Whether we succeed will depend on the toy industry. If we do not, we are in trouble. After all, as the popular expression goes, "Toys R' Us."

12

Grandparents and Grandchildren
The Secret of Redemption

THE MISHNA in *Eduyot* (2:9) makes the following observation in the name of Rabbi Akiva:

> A father endows his son with comely appearance, strength, riches, wisdom, longevity and "*mispar hadorot lefanav*" (the number of generations before him). And this is the secret of redemption, as it says, "He proclaimed the generations from the beginning."
>
> (*Yeshayahu* 41:1)

There is indeed compelling evidence that demonstrates how the genetic code affects the child's physical appearance and intellectual capacity. Economic circumstances, as well as the environment in which a child is reared, also influence much of a person's future. But what is meant by "*mispar hadorot lefanav*, the number of generations before him?"

In this day and age, it is becoming increasingly difficult for successive generations to communicate. The radical innovations which are taking place in technology and science, together with major changes in temperament and outlook, render it nearly impossible for parents to communicate with their children. The generation gap widens all the time; we can foresee the day when parents and children will relate to each other as complete strangers.*

---

* See Rabbi Joseph B. Soloveitchik, *Man of Faith in the Modern World*, vol. 11, Avraham Besdin ed., (Ktav, 1989) ch. 1.

Jews, unlike other nations, have been confronted with this problem many times before. Their history of nearly 4,000 years has served as a constant reminder of the danger of their children losing interest and commitment to their common heritage. Avraham finds difficulties in conveying his mission to his son Yishmael; Yitzchak encounters great problems in getting his message across to his two sons, Yaakov and Esav. Yaakov, himself, does not seem to escape this problem either, and becomes the unintentional initiator of much bitterness between his children, in his seeming preference of one child over the others.

In all these cases, it is misapprehension which causes the breakdown in communication. Words, and even body language and gestures, take on new forms and meanings. This can be clearly demonstrated in the case of the "many colored garment" (*Bereishit* 37) which Yaakov gave to Yosef. According to *Malbim*, this garment was given to Yosef with the explicit purpose of being used only when serving his old father (Yosef was the only one at home). In no way was this gift intended to show any favor to Yosef. The brothers' mind-set, however, was such that they were not able to grasp this and consequently they misread the situation with disastrous consequences. The cultural environment in which the brothers operated, i.e., the society at large, had by now given a different meaning to this kind of gesture.

In exactly the same way, parents today experience great frustration when they suddenly realize that their children completely misunderstand them because they translate their parents' words into their own contemporary language. And the same can be said for parents' misunderstanding of their children.

There seems to be only one way to overcome this problem: by creating a psychological language that finds expression beyond the general cultural and sociological milieu in which children find themselves today. Human beings are indeed profoundly influenced by their surroundings, but, on a deeper level, they seem to carry a kind of psychological gene which is able to build bridges which span many generations. This may be due to what Carl Gustaf Jung spoke of as the "archetype," a kind of a primordial mental image which keeps recurring in a nation and enwraps the human being psychologically into his natural religious inner life (although this was not necessarily Jung's intended meaning). Whatever the component of this gene may be, it will only have a real effect when it is constantly reactivated and relived. This is achieved by ensuring that the past does not become outdated, but if anything "fore-dated." Herein do we discover the purpose of Jewish learning and practice. Jews do not study the past because of what *happened*, but because of what *is* happening, and what will still happen in the future.

In Jewish education, Avraham is not a mythical figure, but an *ever present* inspiration. Jewish students and children experience for themselves his tribulations and his wanderings. They embark with him as he sets off on his journey to Canaan and they tremble when they stand with him on the mountain, as he is about to sacrifice Yitzchak. They flee from home with Yaakov; they share the prison cell with Yosef, and stand next to him when he is appointed second-in-command of Egypt. They accompany Moshe as he leads the Jews into the wilderness, and compose the psalms with King David. Slowly they enter into a world with its own language, they share in the solemnities of the "great ones," dream their dreams and become their companions. There is no longer a generation gap, but a "fraternity of the committed" which surpasses all the superficial pressures and external pulls of society.

Related to this idea, we discover something most fascinating in the life of Yaakov. He seems to relate far better to his grandchildren than to his own children, establishing a most remarkable connection with Ephraim and Menashe. There is no tension and there is no jealousy. He literally bridges the generation gap when he declares to Yosef, "Now your two sons who were born to you in the land of Egypt, before I came to you in Egypt, are mine. Ephraim and Menashe shall be mine, like Reuven and Shimon" (*Bereishit* 48:5). He blesses them, learns with them, and no doubt must have played with them. Indeed Yaakov is called "Yisrael Sava," "Israel the old one," which may also be understood as Yaakov, the grandfather par excellence (*Bereishit Rabbah* 70.1). Why is it that he relates better to his grandchildren than to his children?

We may suggest that this is due to the fact that he only meets his grandchildren at an older age. His trials, tribulations and, above all, his life experiences, have made him into a man of great wisdom. He has learned from his mistakes of youth and inexperience. Now, in his old age, he has developed into a well-balanced person, and it is under these conditions that he meets his grandchildren. The tranquility which he *now* represents transforms him into a great educator. He was unable to offer this to his children, however much he must have loved all of them. It is for this reason that he could not have the same impact on his children as he had, years later, on his grandchildren. His children still saw him in his "raw" state, while his grandchildren saw him as an esteemed and highly distinguished personality. In this way, he became not only the unique grandfather and educator, but also fulfilled the mishnaic statement of "*mispar hadorot lefanav*," connecting the later generations with the earlier ones in an unusual covenant of fraternity. The limitations of time were replaced with the power of eternity. It is not for nothing that the Jewish Tradition requires parents to bless their children with the blessing of a grandfather. It is indeed the secret of redemption.

13

Asterix and Obelix: A Serious Rabbinic View

O NE OF THE GREAT blessings in life, from which many of us benefit, is that we often do not know what we have missed out on. *Ignoti nulla cupido,* "There is no desire for what is not known," said Ovid in his "Ars Amatoria" (III, i.397). This may sound rather strange, but when we examine our own lives we see that many people can be satisfied with their material standard because they do not fully realize, or refuse to realize, that they could have had more.

> The Jewel that we find we stoop and take't
> Because we see it, but what we do not see
> We tread upon, and never think of it.
> (Shakespeare, Measure for Measure
Act II, Scene I.)

Today we have convinced ourselves that we cannot survive without electricity, refrigerators, cars and perhaps even airplanes. We are therefore astonished when we realize that our forefathers lived their lives without any of these "necessities," even though they belonged to the "upper class." We are even more surprised to learn that they were often happier than us. They neither possessed nor missed these belongings for the simple reason that they did not exist.

The famous R. Goscinny and A. Uderzo, in their hilarious cartoons, "Asterix and Obelix"—a parody on modern society which no doubt is well known to our European readers!—tell us in one of their editions, called

"Obelix and Co," about a time when the great emperor, Julius Caesar, was looking for ways to defeat the invincible Gauls. The latter lived in a small town in the north of what was later called France. This small but totally independent village is the home town of the heroes of Asterix and Obelix, who frequently poke fun at the Romans. The Roman army is constantly defeated by the Gauls due to the fact that the latter possess a miraculous potion invented and brewed by the wise Druid, Getafix, which gives the drinker superhuman strength. This is obviously a thorn in the side of Caesar. In a meeting of Caesar's inner cabinet, one most unsympathetic figure suggests that they should try to make the Gauls completely addicted to money so that their interest in warfare and independence will dissipate.

Following this advice, Caesar starts buying thousands of *menhirs*, massive, useless stones, from a company belonging to the Gauls. This company called "Obelix and Co" is run by the Gaul, Obelix. The plan is that Obelix will be seduced by the money he receives, and will thus be forced to employ all his fellow citizens so as to meet the demands of fulfilling Caesar's order. In this way, their attention will be diverted away from warfare, and Caesar will have his way and finally defeat them.

After having acquired a large quantity of these stones, Caesar's treasury is entirely depleted, and he is forced to sell these *menhirs* to his own people before his empire becomes bankrupt. Convincing his citizens to buy these *menhirs* is, however, a major headache. How to convince them of the absolute necessity of possessing these worthless stones?

A major advertisement campaign is launched, and slowly, millions of people start buying these useless stones. Prices rise to absurd levels and the entire Roman empire is convinced that life without these stones is not worth living. Some even contemplate suicide for the lack of them. A whole country is now funded and driven by enormous pieces of stone which have no other function but to get in the way.

While the story is very comical, its message is most serious. Almost nothing will be missed unless it has once been tasted. A person only feels deprived of something once he or she are aware of its existence, or when they have experienced it even for a very short period of time.

Cartoons have proved to be a remarkably effective means of communicating profound ideas. While we do not wish to equate the Torah with cartoons, our sages did teach us that God created the world in such a way that spiritual circumstances are represented in the secular realm. In this way, the profane holds a spark of that which takes place in the world of holiness.

When appointing Aharon and his sons to the priesthood in the *Mishkan*, Moshe is told by God: "And you shall let Aharon your brother and his sons with him come near to you from among the children of Israel that they minister unto Me as priests...." (*Shemot* 28:1)

Most unusual is the expression "come near to you" (*hakrev*). We would have expected that the text would read "and you shall appoint Aharon and his sons." *Ohr HaChayim*, the great eighteenth-century commentator on the Torah, reminds us of the fact that it was originally God's plan to have Moshe himself be the high priest. But since Moshe refused to respond to God's request at the Burning Bush (see *Shemot* 3), to take full responsibility as leader and redeemer of the people of Israel, the task to become the high priest (in addition to being the leader) was denied to him and transferred to his brother Aharon (see *Shemot Rabbah* 3.17).

Most surprising, however, is the fact that Moshe *did* become the high priest, albeit for a short time. The Torah informs us, in the aforementioned chapter, that *for seven days* Moshe functioned as the high priest in the newly built *Mishkan*. Only then was Moshe asked to pass the priesthood on to Aharon, his brother. This requires an explanation. Why was the priesthood not *immediately* given to Aharon, as was already decided at the time of the Burning Bush? *Ohr HaChayim* provides us with a powerful answer. He claims that God decided on this procedure to remind Moshe of what he had lost when he hesitated in complying with His request at the Burning Bush. By making Moshe a high priest for only a few days, God gave him a taste of the greatness, dignity and merit of this office.

It is for this reason that he was asked to make sure that Aharon and his sons "come near" ("*hakrev*") to him to become the new priests. The word "*hakrev*" has a double meaning, says *Ohr HaChayim*. It means "to bring near" but it is also related to the word "*korban*." Moshe was asked by God to bring a sacrifice as a *kapara*, an atonement, for his earlier refusal, by giving the priesthood over to his brother after one week of office. He would not have known what he had lost had he not first tasted what it meant to be a high priest. This, says *Ohr HaChayim*, is the great sacrifice which Moshe brought.

It should be understood that the sacrifice that Moshe had to undergo was not necessarily a punishment for his failure to appreciate what was offered to him, but was a message to future generations that a person has to learn to carefully contemplate and appreciate what is offered to him before he rejects it. Only when one recognizes the extent of one's loss will one appreciate what one could have had. Indeed, "*Ignoti nulla cupido.*"

– 14 –

The Therapy of Sport

THE NEED TO ENGAGE in sport is self-evident. To exercise and to make sure that one keeps one's body in good condition is considered a *mitzva* of the highest priority.

Still, there is little evidence to suggest that Jews in earlier centuries were ever seriously involved in sport. No doubt this is due to the historical conditions of the period of the Second Temple. With the conquest of the land of Israel by Alexander the Great (fourth century BCE), Hellenist culture began to infiltrate, and the attempts of Antiochus Epiphanes to Hellenize Judea led to the outbreak of the war of the Maccabees. When this caused some Jews to take measures to conceal the fact that they were circumcised—because they had to appear naked in the Greek gymnasia—the opposition by Judaism towards Hellenism increased, and so sport, which was traditionally identified with the Greeks, became a taboo activity. This became even more apparent when the Olympic Games were connected with idolatrous cults, particularly of the Greek deity, Hercules.

Little information is provided in the Talmud about sport, except that it informs us that one was allowed to go to the Greek stadia while gladiatorial games took place "to shout so as to save the life of a victim" (*Avoda Zara* 18b). This was indeed exceptional as the sages ordinarily forbade the attendance of such events as theatrical performances, circuses and athletic competitions, since these events were used to make mockery of Jews and Judaism, and often involved unethical and cruel practices. The famous sage and *Amora*, Resh Lakish was, in his earlier days, a professional gladiator, but abandoned this activity when he became attracted to Judaism (*Gittin* 47a). Most interesting is the dispute between Rabbi Yosef Karo, the author of the *Shulchan Aruch*, and Rabbi Moshe Isserles, over whether one is allowed to play ball on Shabbat and festivals (*Orach Chaim* 308.45; 518.2). Only in modern times have Jews become more actively involved in sport.

Millions of people are under the false impression that they are sportsmen simply because they *watch* a game. This is most remarkable. Tens of thousands of people become completely mesmerized in front of the television screen as they watch a ball being kicked around by twenty-two players. The fact that these people are prepared to run around like crazy for the benefit of thousands is a topic which should keep psychologists busy for a long time.

Even more fascinating is the fact that the thousands sitting in the stands shake their heads in approval or disapproval while shouting pieces of advice to the players. They play the "experts," with the attitude that they should be on the field themselves, since their expertise in football is "obviously" far superior to "those amateurs" on the field.

What is the secret behind this? Watching a game of sport has obviously nothing to do with sport. *It is therapy.* Many human beings have to go to work and be submissive themselves to their employers. They cannot tell their bosses what they really think of them. When they shout at the soccer player, informing him that he is a *shlemiel*, and that he does not know how to handle the ball, they are really shouting at their boss. It brings tremendous relief, allowing one to vent one's pent up frustration. One is able to abandon the artificial courtesy which one is obliged to show at work. Human beings need this release.

There are, however, other dimensions to sport which should demand our full attention. Psychologists have not yet been able to fully explain such sports as tobogganing and skiing. Upon further thought, we must admit that there is something most bizarre about these sports. It is difficult to understand why people are prepared to climb a mountain for over an hour, leaving themselves in a breathless and sweaty state, only to undo this in a matter of a few minutes by hurtling down the same mountain. This is almost discouraging. It reminds us of Sisyphus, the famous personality in Greek mythology, who was doomed to roll a heavy stone up a mountain. Every time he slipped, he had to start all over again. It makes us wonder: for Sisyphus this was torment, for us it is a winter sport! We must conclude that a human being is prepared to torment him/herself as long as they convince themselves that it is sport. This, again, should captivate the full attention of psychologists.

Some Perspectives on Mortality

In *Devarim* (14:1), the Torah warns against excessive mourning, expressing itself in a most unusual way: "You are the children of the Lord, your God, you shall not cut yourself, nor make a bald patch between your eyes for the dead." This prohibition teaches Man the correct approach towards death.

The great sixteenth-century sage, Ovadia Sforno, explains this in his own unique way: the reason why one is not allowed to mourn excessively is because a more noble Relative is still alive. And since one is a child of that Relative, and He is the ultimate Father, one knows that the real Parent did not die and never will die. So, if one excessively grieves, it is as if one believes that not even *the* Parent is left alive. As such, "absolute" mourning is proscribed. (See also the *Da'at Baalei Tosafot*.)

There is a great difference between mourning for one's parents when one is an adult or still a child. In the case of an adult, the loss is less selfish because most adults no longer depend on their parents in the same way that children do. In this sense, the obligation to honor one's parents takes on a higher quality, with more dignity and altruistic intentions. There is more room for genuine interest in the parent as a unique human being whose child one happens to be. Once the life of a parent comes to an end, and passes on to another world, there is a greater chance for contemplation about the meaning of life and the uniqueness of those who left us behind. This is the main reason for the period of "*shiva*," the seven days intensive mourning period following burial, when one is not allowed to work, and is required to sit low (nearly on the floor), serving as a reminder of our earthliness.

Death confronts us with a strange paradox. We realize that all of us have been longer dead than alive. Before we were born, we were "dead" for "millions" of years. Somehow, on a subconscious level, we are better acquainted with our existence prior to life than when we find ourselves thrust quite suddenly into this world.

Real life is a journey which starts long before we come into existence. It seems to come from afar and progresses along its way through experience, growth, suffering, insight and deed, only to then return to its home base. There is an eternal continuum which seems to precede the existence of the individual, and the journey of life continues after death.

This world is like a busy station with many travelers coming and going. Every day, hundreds of thousands leave and travel to "home base," and simultaneously, thousands upon thousands of others arrive from that very base to spend some time at this station. If it would be possible for a person to view, from above, this highway between heaven and earth, he would be surprised how heavy the daily traffic is in both directions. There are those who embark upon an outing, perhaps not knowing what awaits them, and there are those who come home, perhaps not realizing what they are leaving behind.

When confronted with death, our first reaction is consternation. We are stunned and broken. But, slowly, our feeling of shock makes room for a sensation of mystery. The *mysterium magnum* enters, and a new perspective emerges which is a kind of revelation and elevation. Suddenly our whole life, which up until this point we knew so well, slowly but surely becomes concealed behind a great Secret. Our speech is silenced. Our understanding fails. There is only awe for the Other.

In the Torah, nobody dies. Rather one is "gathered to his fathers." No *neshama* becomes dust, and no spirit turns into ashes. *Neshamot* compose immortal and untouchable words, and create infinite art and abstract thoughts. As such, the *neshama* is infinite. Friedrich Nietzsche said: "The final reward of the dead is to die no more." Judaism would say: the final reward of the dead is to not see death anymore.

The *Halacha* makes a distinction between mourning for deceased parents and other members of one's family. While one mourns for a parent for a full year, this is not the case with any other member of the family, not even for one's spouse.

There is something very distinctive about parents. No doubt it has to do with the fact that one can have more children, brothers or sisters, and even marry another wife, but one can never have other parents. They are irreplaceable. But on a deeper level, parents are our bond with earlier generations; they are our links with bygone days. They are our memory, and they provide us with the historical and emotional context to our lives. Rabbi Yitschak Hutner, *z"l*, once remarked that we have a full year of mourning for our parents because, unlike in the other cases where we lose family members, the loss of a parent removes us even further from the days of the revelation of the Torah at Sinai. Only through a year of mourning, i.e., a period of meditation and *teshuva*, are we able to recapture this great moment.

– 16 –

Religious and Secular Morality

W<small>HEN DISCUSSING MATTERS</small> related to the ethical or religious foundation of sexual behavior, people tend to have severe differences of opinion. While up until the second half of the twentieth century, a more conservative approach was still prevailing, a radical change occurred in the second half of the last century.

Well-established norms were suddenly challenged, and often replaced, by radical approaches which demanded greater "liberty" and "broadmindedness." This provoked a major confrontation between the conservatives and those who claimed that they were "modern-minded."

Since those days, we have witnessed many debates surrounding such topics as homosexuality, same-sex marriages and abortion. Both sides try to prove their point of view with learned dissertations and elaborate arguments.

But those who survey this literature have long since been convinced that such debates will lead nowhere. There is no reconciliation nor any *modus vivendi* which will bring these camps any closer. The reason is obvious: there is no common ground that could serve as a platform for constructive discussion. In the Mishna in *Chagiga* (2.1) we are confronted with several educational problems related to the esoteric world. The Mishna asks: How many people are permitted to be present when a teacher lectures on matters "beyond"? It concludes that some issues, such as the secrets of Creation (*Ma'asei Bereishit*), should only be taught to one person at a time, while other metaphysical topics, such as the ones mentioned in the book of *Yechezkel* (the *Merkava*, the celestial world), should only be taught by a sage of great wisdom and also only in front of one pupil. The main reason given for these rulings is to prevent misunderstandings. When only one student at a time is present, there will be little chance that the student will misunderstand his mentor. He will be forced to listen carefully to every word the teacher speaks. There is no luxury of dozing off, of only hearing half of the lecture and drawing the wrong conclusions.

At the opening of the same Mishna, we are informed that matters of *arayot* (sexuality and its prohibitions) should not be taught to more than *two* students at a time. The reason for this "lenient" rule (i.e., that two students are permitted to learn simultaneously) is that both students will make sure that they hear all that is said about sexuality, since most human beings are preoccupied with the subject. Even when the teacher is only speaking to one of them, the other one will also listen. Three, however, is seen to be a problematic number, since the other two may start a discussion among themselves, draw the wrong conclusions and permit what is forbidden or vice versa.

The *Maharsha*, however, gives a completely different interpretation regarding the nature of rules related to sexuality. According to him, these rules are also completely mysterious, and belong in the same category as *Ma'asei Bereishit* and the esoteric observations concerning the metaphysical world by the prophet Yechezkel. No explanation is available as to why certain sexual relationships are forbidden and others are permitted. The *Maharsha* asks, for example, why marrying one's sister is prohibited. He also questions why men are prohibited from marrying their living wife's sister, but are allowed to marry the same sister after their wife has died (see *Vayikra* 18). (According to the Torah one is allowed to marry a second wife; it was the sages who forbade this in later days.)

To claim that any of the prohibited relationships are fundamentally "unethical" is untenable, for the obvious reason that the children of Adam and Chava married their brothers and sisters. Nowhere is it written that this was forbidden. In fact, it was the only way that God saw fit to increase the human species. Similarly we see that Yaakov married two sisters, something that later became prohibited. Furthermore, as is well known, these marriages laid the foundation stone of the Jewish people and were indispensable!

It is for this reason, says *Maharsha*, that one should only teach these matters to two pupils at a time so as to prevent any false explanation. The nature of the rules of sexuality are so complex that two students might possibly start arguing amongst themselves while the mentor might only be concentrating on the third. They would advance all sorts of explanations, claim that they found the raison d'être of the subject, and go on to permit or forbid all sorts of marriages.

Maharsha's observation is therefore of primary importance. All discussions of *why* certain marriages or sexual relationships are forbidden are doomed to fail! No human reasoning is able to explain them in any consistent way. It is for this reason that religious thinkers should distance themselves from giving primary reasons for these prohibitions. It would be counter-productive and dangerous. This is true when discussing homosexuality or other forbidden relationships. Although some of these relationships have been forbidden since the days of the creation of Man, these prohibitions are still beyond human comprehension and should be accepted as such.

It is here that a difficulty arises for secular philosophy and ethics. On the basis of which *rational* principle should a homosexual relationship be permitted but incest forbidden?

However unsavory our argument may sound, we are forced to ask what could be wrong, from a secular perspective, with incest, fetishism, or bestiality? As long as such a relationship takes place by mutual consent, and nobody gets physically or mentally hurt, there should be no reason why these relationships should be forbidden. While several philosophers have attempted to apply rational reasons for why such acts should be prohibited by secular law, we have to conclude that no consistent and rational argument has yet been put forward which is fundamentally sound.

Arguments such as the "need for human dignity" are meaningless, because it is unclear how one defines human dignity, and even when it is clear, it could be asked why it should be an absolute inviolable value.

We are therefore forced to conclude that when secular law forbids certain sexual acts, it borrows values from a system which is alien to its own philosophy. The secular understanding of sexual morality does not make any sense unless one admits that it is founded on religious premises. Religious thinkers, however, should not forget, as *Maharsha* pointed out, that religious philosophy is also unable to provide an explanation for these laws.

These prohibitions cannot be the result of rational deduction or ethical contemplation, but must be rooted in a "will" which is external to Man. Either one accepts this external will or one rejects it. Once one rejects such an external will, there can be no distinction made between matters such as homosexuality and incest, and as such, both relationships should be permitted.

One is reminded of the words of Professor E. S. Waterhouse:

A parasite is an independent organism, but its existence is nonetheless dependent upon its host. If the host perishes, the parasite perishes with it. Using the term in the scientific and not in an offensive way, may not morality which is not dependent of religion be parasitic upon the religious system within which it has grown up? Surely the question of morality independent of religion cannot be settled by reference to individuals whose moral life began in a community saturated with ideas of religion.

("The Religious Basis of Morality" in Essays presented to J. H. Hertz, London, 1942, pp. 413–14)

Richard Livingstone in *Education for a World Adrift* adds: "We have inherited good habits and habits persist almost indefinitely, if there is nothing to destroy them. A plant may continue in apparent health for some time after its roots have been cut, but its days are numbered" (London, 1941, p. 24).

It is, therefore, abundantly clear that secular society ultimately depends on religious values. It is time that secular thinkers become honest enough to admit this, however painful the truth may be.

– 17 –

Satisfaction and the Art of Being

And the time of threshing shall reach until the vintage and the vintage shall reach the sowing time. You shall eat your bread to satiety and you shall dwell in your land without worry.

(*Vayikra* 26:5)

This blessing is promised to the people of Israel when, as a united nation, it observes the Law of the Torah and lives by its spirit. Its promise is quite surprising. Not only will the Israelites have plenty to eat but, as the verse clearly indicates, the Jews will experience an overflow of food. The first season, when produce is brought to the threshing floor, will last until the days of the vineyard, these days, will in turn continue into the days of sowing.

Rashi, the great French commentator, quoting *Torat Cohanim*, makes an extraordinary statement, informing us that the verse is teaching us that one will "eat a little, and it will be blessed in his innards." He seems to understand this verse in an entirely different way from what one would have imagined. It appears that it is *not* the quantity of food which will increase, but the *quality*. The food consumed will be of such a high quality that eating only a small amount will produce the same benefit as would eating a large amount in a year which is not specially blessed.

The explanation of the verse, as understood by *Torat Cohanim* and Rashi, would then indicate that very little food will be consumed by people throughout the year so that the same amount of food normally consumed in a short period of time will now last much longer. Thus, the time of threshing will hold enough food until the vintage, etc.

There is, however, a completely different way of looking at this verse which may carry great meaning for our days. The famous thinker and teacher of *Mussar*, Rabbi Yerucham of the Mir Yeshiva in Poland (twentieth century) alludes to an even greater miracle which our verse mentions (see *Mussarei HaTorah*). This time, it is not the quality of the *food* but the quality of *Man* which makes the difference.

According to Rabbi Yerucham, there will be no difference between a year which is blessed and one which is not. Both will produce the same amount and also the same quality of food. What will change is Man's *attitude* to his physical possessions.

To be satisfied and happy is the greatest blessing which can ever be bestowed on Man. But such a blessing has absolutely no relation to the *amount* of food or possessions which Man happens to eat or own. The Torah teaches us that when the people of Israel live in accordance with the requirements of the Torah, Man will be blessed with a frame of mind in which matters of possession and food will take on a completely different dimension. This attitude is not something which an individual can develop independently, but will only arise as a result of his receptiveness towards the Divine and God's response. When a person has achieved high moral and spiritual latitudes, they will see the world in a very different light. After one's basic needs are fulfilled, one will see oneself as what Erich Fromm calls a "be-ing," i.e., one who will "be-come," and one who sees one's essence in one's spiritual growth (Erich Fromm, *To Have or To Be*, Abacus, 1976). It is not what person "has," but what he "is" which is of real importance. At such a moment, satisfaction is no longer the result of *possessing* more, but of "*being*" more.

It is most remarkable that the Torah emphasizes that it is, first and foremost, our mind-set which allows for this state of "being." Judaism was the first to postulate that mental health and sickness are outcomes of right and wrong living. When people are greedy or ambitious to attain fame, we hold them in contempt because we believe that they have the wrong kind of thoughts. The Torah, however, teaches us that without denying other possible causes, they actually suffer from a kind of mental illness which is the outcome of *immoral action*.

This also relates to the concept of joy. Joy is concomitant to productive activity. It is not a peak experience which ends suddenly, but rather a plateau which is the product of one's essential human faculties. It is not the ecstatic fire of the moment, but the glow that accompanies "being." It is only with this type of true joy that one is able to be satisfied with the minimum while experiencing it to the maximum.

iii. A Fairy Tale

King Democratio: A Modern Midrash*

Once upon a time, in a large, gloomy palace, high on a mountain, where the night wind howled outside its massive walls, there lived a king—a real one. His beard was long like a silver waterfall, and his voice boomed like thunder. More than that, a king does not need. His name was Teuton, though some called him Germania. Wherever he traveled, his citizens would grovel before him in the dust, and if they failed to do so, they were knocked into it anyway. You see, O reader, how mighty our king was.

In the course of time, King Teuton produced a son called Democratio. This prince had one remarkable feature—he possessed a hollow head. It was completely empty. There was nothing between his ears, absolutely nothing. It is hard for us to grasp this idea because our heads are so full. (Though were they otherwise, we would find it even harder.) For a long time even the prince himself was not aware of his peculiarity. For one thing, he could not tell that his head was empty precisely because it was empty. And for another, nobody could let him know, because it was impossible to tell, just by looking at him, how empty his head really was—a real stroke of luck! And, most of all, nobody would have dared to tell him, because it is not wise to tell the king's son the truth unless, of course, it is pleasant.

But the truth will out. One day, when the prince was thirteen, he went running pell-mell up the stairs and banged his right royal head against a wooden beam. It rang audibly, just like an empty champagne glass. The prince

---

* This story is my thorough adaptation of a story published by the well-known Dutch author Godfried J. A. Bomans.

was most surprised. He tapped gingerly on the side of his skull and indeed it gave a light, clear echo. "Dear me!" exclaimed the astonished prince, "Could my head, this valuable head of state, really be empty?" He hurried to the physician of the royal household. Now, the physician was a wise man.

"Examine this head," commanded the prince, and so the wise physician did. It was a tricky task indeed to tell the prince the truth about his head, especially because he wanted to keep his own. But, as I mentioned, the physician was a very wise man. He took his small silver hammer and tapped gently on the important head. It made a clear, beautiful, empty sound.

"Your majesty," the physician announced, "I congratulate you. It is quite empty."

"Really?" said the prince, suddenly very pleased, "is it really hollow?"

"Oh yes, sire," and the physician bowed low. "It is extremely rare, and especially with such a magnificent sound!"

"But," said the king's son, suddenly worried, "when my wicked father dies, then I shall have to reign. How can I with an empty head?"

The physician tiptoed silently to the door and locked it. He bent towards the royal ear and whispered: "Thou hast a most unique head to reign! Whenever there is a conflict of opinion in the land, do as follows: Listen first to one party and send it away."

"All right," said the prince.

"Then hear the other party and send it away as well."

"Fine," said the prince.

"That is all," said the physician, smiling.

"But," asked the prince, "which party is right?"

The physician carefully looked around to make sure that nobody could hear and quickly replied: "The larger."

❧

Cruel old King Teuton died. It was a marvelous day of flag-waving and rejoicing; but amidst all the festivities, the nervous new king came to the throne with a heart full of foreboding. But he needn't have worried. In fact, he managed to the satisfaction of nearly everyone present. The reputation of his wisdom rapidly spread beyond the country's borders, and the secret of his hollow head stayed right in that head, which shows, dear reader, how easy it is to hide nothing!

One fine day, the king made a great dinner. I cannot begin to tell you how magnificent this feast was. It was of such stately extravagance that even the British participants were impressed. It was a spectacle of incredible proportions. The tables were laden with the most expensive gold cutlery and the finest bone china. The aristocracy trod softly and in awe as though the Messiah himself was expected to attend. There was soft music, so gentle that it could barely be heard; but on the other hand, its absence would have been noticed. Few words were spoken, little was eaten. After all, the guests were too refined to show their base inclinations. The conversations, although quite meaningless, were held in the most refined Latin. In short, a delightful evening, even by the standards of the nobility. King Democratio could hardly contain his delight. His glittering eyes revealed his great satisfaction. Such a success with an empty head!

Then, by chance, the king glanced into the reception hall. His expression became suddenly severe. Standing at the entrance of the palace door was an old, dusty man gasping for breath.

"Hey," called the king, waving his scepter, "what is this?"

"Sire, Sire...."

"What?" called the king, warily edging closer to the man.

"A crisis, Sire," he exclaimed. "A crisis has come over the land."

"A what?" asked the king.

"A crisis, Sire...."

"Well," said the king, "that is bad." He did not know what a crisis was, but he understood that it was something sad, and therefore he looked as a king should look at such a moment.

"This is a great pity," he declared, and in his heart grew a great malaise.

The next morning, when the king awoke in his stately bed, he stared up at the satin canopy and thought about the crisis. What a pity it had to come and spoil everything. It had all been going so well despite his empty head. "First of all," he said to himself, "I have to find out what a crisis is." He dressed quickly and summoned all the wise men of the land. They came. Majestically, they walked through the streets to the palace, their long beards flowing before them, sighing under the weight of their wisdom. Some of them had heads so heavy with wisdom that they nearly tumbled off their shoulders in front of the curious populace! You can understand what a deep impression this made.

They told the king the meaning of a crisis. It took three days before they finished, though barely a few minutes had passed before the eyes of the king were filled with tears, since his heart was good and compassionate. He listened carefully for three days. Then the wise men fell silent.

"Are you finished?" asked the king.

"Yes, Sire," the wise men said, "that is all."

They straightened their beards and left. And the king sat on his throne alone. Evening came, and the king still sat in the darkness and thought and thought and began to cry—a small, sad figure.

❦

Confusion and emotion seized the country. There had to be a solution! First, there came a royal decree to write as many books as possible about the crisis, a command to anybody who could wield a pen. The books did not have to be completely true, but they did have to be fat and cheap. There also had to be many, many meetings, each with at least two speakers, an introductory discussion, a concluding debate, a vote of thanks and, if possible, a word of sincere tribute. Filled with courage, the citizens began their work. As far as the books were concerned, the nation split into two working groups, those who wrote about the disaster and those who read about it, agreeing with the authors how disastrous the disaster really was. But most of the time was spent at the meetings. Evening after evening, the citizens listened, applauded and asked intelligent questions.

The king himself worked even harder. He did nothing but read what was written, wading through the growing mountain of literature from early in the morning until late at night. He spent the whole day in pajamas; there was no time to dress. He learned what money was, who owned it, who did not own it, and who should own it. He learned about workmen, and how they worked. He learned the laws of supply and demand, of prices and value, and an amazing thing began to happen! Slowly his head filled up. It gradually became heavier and heavier as the crumbs of wisdom collected and combined, until it was completely filled.

"And now," said the king, "we shall apply all that we have learned."

Laws began to spew forth from the palace. Good laws, intelligent laws, refined laws. But the incredible happened. The crisis remained. The misery grew, and the citizens became impatient. The king was not as wise as some had thought! And when the king heard of all this, he laughed and proclaimed new laws, even more intelligent, more refined and sophisticated. But still the misery kept growing. The king grew a beard, and his beard became gray. Every night he lay in bed awake, tossing and turning, slowly going mad. Until, one night, he suddenly sat bolt upright. Struck by a blinding flash of inspiration, he shook his head in wonder, marveling at his own wisdom. Then he lay down again and slept a pleasant sleep.

The next day, royal couriers on horses hastened into the neighboring countries; they blew on brass trumpets and sang a great song: "The king has found a solution."

One hundred and twenty monarchs were invited to Democratio's kingdom. One hundred and twenty mighty kings came to put everything in order in one enormous meeting. Flags were hoisted, and people came into the streets to see the mighty kings. There they were! Kings came from the east, west, north and south. Only one king was not invited. His territory was too small, and one could do without him. So all the great kings gathered. After appearing on the palace balcony, where they met with a rapturous welcome from the crowds, they withdrew to deliberate. Each king naturally had a vast retinue of chroniclers, scholars and private secretaries who formed themselves into upper-committees, middle-committees and lower-committees. These were divided into main-committees, and these again into sub-committees, that were again divided into bodies of legal advisers, sub-advisers and sub-sub-advisers. It became an enormous writing crowd. At the end of this momentous day, King Democratio gave his people a few words of reassurance from his royal balcony and the populace went to bed, satisfied.

The next morning, the one hundred and twenty kings rose early, ate a quick breakfast, and carried on, creating sub-sub-sub committees. In this fashion, many days passed until the web of committees became so complicated and intricate that further branching became impossible. In the meantime, King Democratio had become very tired. Each evening he came out to his balcony to reassure his good people of progress, and, in fact, there were special people appointed to produce papers throughout the land in which the reassuring words were printed.

But this terrible tale of woe gets no better. All the king's words and all the papers were of no avail. The crisis remained and indeed further deteriorated. King Democratio could no longer continue. His beard went totally white. He met with the sub-committees and the sub-sub-committees. He told the authors of the papers about their responsibilities. He dined with the kings. And, most difficult of all, he kept on speaking about the fantastic results of the conference, which would no doubt lead to a solution.

But his eyes were sad, his hands were white, and they trembled. And the people began to grumble, slowly but surely, like tormented creatures. They expected bread, but in return received only papers and strange statements. One evening they began to gather in a crowd under the royal balcony—stark, silent, pinched faces. Soldiers came and dispersed the crowds. The next evening they came back. The soldiers were cruel, and the people were tortured. But they still came from all directions, more and more people, forming an enormous crowd. They called out for the kings. They wanted to see the kings. So the kings came out onto the balcony. Thousands of fists were raised, a powerful cry rose from the crowds and the kings stood with bowed heads. They tried to speak, but they were not heard. They asked for silence, but there was no response. Then one sharp voice raised itself above the tumult of the people:

"There was another king who was not invited!"

King Democratio peered down over the balcony. "And who is *that*?" he asked mockingly.

The crowd was silent for a moment, then the same voice called:

"You kings, fools, jesters of wisdom and intellect, who gave you your crowns on your heads and ermine on your shoulders?"

And the one hundred and twenty kings fell silent.

The lonely voice had spoken: "We, with all our one hundred and twenty kings, are powerless if one more King is not invited."

And dear reader, if you will ask why some kings, thousands of years ago, managed so successfully, remember that they invited the other King as well....

iv. Man, God and the Torah

– 19 –

Who is God and
What Are the Consequences?

Who is god? This question is perhaps the most difficult of all to answer. It is like being asked to explain a three-dimensional reality with the help of a flat surface. Still, God is the most captivating Figure in human history and His track record is most unusual. His deeds are unprecedented, but often very disturbing. He is to be loved, but often irritates. He is above all human limitation, but He becomes angry and outright emotional. He is beyond criticism, but is judged by the strictest criteria of justice.

Religious people and thinkers believe that He is the only One who really has it all together and knows what He is doing. But others are convinced that He is absentminded, lets things get out of hand, and causes unnecessary pain to some of His creatures. No figure has ever been the cause of so much controversy, shuddering silence and admiration.

No one is so conspicuous while using an ingenious hideout called the universe. While God is the great mystery in a person's life, some human beings have a relationship with Him as if He is their best friend, with whom they can converse and to whom they can complain. He is the personal psychologist of millions of people but is ultimately blamed for anything that goes wrong. Who is this strange figure called God? Most important is to realize that the term God is used arbitrarily. It often stands for completely opposing entities used by religious and quasi-religious ideologies. All of them agree that "God" affirms some Absolute Reality as the Ultimate. But they fundamentally disagree as to what that reality is all about. For Benedictus Spinoza, the Dutch philosopher and Jewish apostate who lived in the seventeenth century, and other pantheistic thinkers, God is really an "It," a primal, impersonal force, identical with all nature—some ineffable, immutable, impassive, Divine substance that pervades the universe or *is* the universe. God is only immanent. He is permanently pervading the universe but He is not transcendent. A Divine spirit which has little practical meaning in an individual's day-to-day life.

This is not so for Judaism and other monotheistic religions. For the Jewish Tradition God is not an idea or just a blind force, but the *Ribono shel Olam*, Master of the Universe, who, besides being its Creator and immanent, is also transcendent, surpassing the universe. He has the disturbing habit of being anywhere and everywhere, and He is known to interfere with anything and everything. He is a *living* God who is a dynamic power in the life and history of Man, moving things around when He sees fit, and smiling or getting annoyed with His creatures when they have blundered yet again.

But, most importantly, while He does not fit into any category, He has, for the lack of a better word, "personality" and His own consciousness. His essence cannot be *expressed*, but He can definitely be *addressed*.

This radical difference in the conception of God makes for an equally profound divergence in attitudes about all life and the universe. While in pantheistic and other non-monotheistic philosophies, He has no moral input, nothing could be further from the Jewish concept of God. For Judaism, He is the source par excellence of all moral criteria.

According to pantheism and the like, the world is eternal, without a beginning. As such, it does not have a purpose, since purpose is the *conscious* motivation of a creator to bring something into existence. It therefore follows that in the pantheistic view, Man cannot have any purpose either. He, like the universe, just "is," and, so, moral behavior may have some utilitarian purpose but no ultimate one. For pantheism, it is not the *goal* of Man to be moral; morality is simply a *means* to his survival. Would moral behavior no longer be needed as a means for Man to survive, it could be dispensed with. On a deeper level, the pantheistic world view sees the universe as an illusion—an unreal, shifting flux of sensory deception. As such, it should be ignored and escaped from. Made from a purely spiritual substance, it could not accommodate any physical reality and, therefore, could not have any real meaning. Neither could Man. Once his physical existence is branded as an illusion, he can no longer exist as "a man of flesh and blood." Nor are his deeds of any real value. Since it is the body which gives Man the opportunity to act, and Man's body is seen as part of the deception, it must follow that all of Man's behavior belongs to the world of illusion as well. It is this view that Judaism contests.

God is a conscious Being who created the world with a purpose. And this world is real, and is by no means a mirage. Man's deeds, far from being an illusion, are of great value; they are the *very goal* of creation. Judaism objects to the pantheistic view of Man since it depersonalizes him, an act which must finally lead to his *demoralization*. If Man is part of an illusion, so are his feelings. So why be concerned with a fellow human being's emotional and physical welfare?

Paradoxically, this pantheism infiltrated Western culture via the back door. When we are told by certain modern philosophers that Man is *only* physical, and his body a scientific mechanism in which emotions are just a chemical inconvenience, we are confronted with a kind of pantheism that is turned on its head. While pantheism denies the physical side of existence, this so-called scientific approach rejects the spiritual dimension of Man. In both cases, emotions are seen as being part of an illusion, and are therefore to be ignored.

Judaism, on the other hand, declares that emotions are what make Man into Man, and that they are real and of crucial importance. In fact, emotions are central to Man's existence since they are the foundation of moral behavior. While pantheism teaches that moral criteria belong to the veil of illusion, Judaism declares them to be vital. It is for that reason that Judaism views God as an emotional being. By giving God, metaphorically speaking, emotions, these feelings are elevated to a supreme state. If God Himself has emotions such as love, mercy, jealousy and anger, then they *must* be real and serious, and should not be ignored when found in Man.

While some philosophers considered such anthropomorphism as scandalous, the Jewish Tradition took the risk of granting God emotions so as to uphold morality on its highest level and guarantee it would not be tampered with. For the sake of Man, even God is prepared to compromise His absolute Otherness, albeit not to the point that He would be projected as a human being.

It was the great gentile philosopher Ludwig Wittgenstein who pointed to the inherent danger in Western society in which God became makeshift. While the vast majority of mankind in the western hemisphere declares that it believes in God, this majority seems to add two more words to its declaration of faith. Instead of saying: "I believe in God," it states: "I believe in God, *so what?*" In such a way, the most radical encounter which Man could ever have with the Master of the Universe has been minimized to a senseless blur of insincerity. Against this Judaism protests. *God is of no importance unless He is of supreme importance.*

20

The Holiness of Man

THERE IS NO DOUBT that an unfaltering commitment to human dignity is the foundation stone of Judaism. This is normally understood to mean that since the Torah includes many commandments in which Man is asked to uphold and guarantee the dignity of his fellow individual, it serves as a proof of God's ongoing love and respect for Man. This is one of the highest values granted to Man.

A careful reading of a comment made by the eighteenth century *Chatam Sofer* seems, however, to suggest a completely different and most unique interpretation of the above idea. In the book of *Shemot* (31:13), we are reminded of one of the most important laws regulating Man's relationship to God: the institution of the Shabbat rest. This law, as no other, reflects Man's obligation towards God. Man is asked to suspend his dominion over the world (by withdrawing from work) and give evidence that all of creation belongs to its Creator, including Man Himself.

Before introducing the commandments related to the building of the *Mishkan*, God tells Moshe:

> But ("*Ach*") My *Shabbatot* you shall keep. For that is a sign between Me and you throughout the generations that you may know that I, God, sanctify you.
>
> (*Shemot* 31:13)

Ramban, unlike Rashi, points out that the word, "But" ("*Ach*"), limits the need to observe the Shabbat and teaches us that in certain cases one *should* violate Shabbat. This is due to the fact that the Hebrew expression "*ach*" in talmudic tradition always limits a general rule stated in a verse. A more correct translation therefore should be: "But, *with certain exceptions*, you shall keep My *Shabbatot*."

The most famous case of such an exception is the one related to saving a human life on Shabbat. When a human being's life is in danger, the law actually requires the violation of Shabbat so as to save this life. Failure to do so would be a clear transgression of God's Torah.

At the same time we also know that it is forbidden to build the *Mishkan* on Shabbat (see *Shemot* 22). This, according to Ramban, is learned from the fact that the Torah *first* discusses the importance of observing the Shabbat, and only *then* goes on to discuss the way in which the *Mishkan* needs to be built.

Because of this, *Chatam Sofer* concludes that although the *Mishkan* is of tremendous importance and holiness (as a symbol of God's indwelling in this world, a kind of "holiness in *space*"), the institution of Shabbat, "holiness in *time*," is even greater and, therefore, more sacred. However, since we are obligated to violate the Shabbat so as to save somebody's life, we see that human life is holier than Shabbat and the *Mishkan*.

We may suggest a most novel interpretation: God seems to be saying to Man: Do you know why I gave you a *Mishkan* and the institution of the Shabbat? This is *not* because they are a goal in themselves, and to teach how holy they are, but so as to teach you how holy *you* are! This is clearly the meaning of the end of the verse: "so that you may know that I, God, sanctify *you*!" Without the instruction to build the *Mishkan*, and the commandment concerning the need to observe Shabbat, Man would never have known *how* holy he actually is! More holy than the *Mishkan* or Shabbat!

This then opens a new perspective: the supreme goal of those laws which regulate and inspire Man to relate to God, and to give evidence to His ultimate authority, is to teach Man to realize his *own* holiness and that of *his neighbor*. This is a completely novel way of grasping the Jewish traditional teachings concerning the dignity of Man.

21

Freud and Belief in God

Sigmund freud, the originator of psychoanalysis, and a figure comparable in importance to Galileo and Einstein, devoted a great deal of attention to religion. His works such as *Totem and Taboo* (1913), *The Future of an Illusion* (1927), and *Moses and Monotheism* (1939), reveal his unusual interest in religion and in particular the psychological reasons for human religiosity.

Freud, however, did not have one good word to say about religion. He regarded religious beliefs as "…illusions, fulfillments of the oldest, strongest and most insistent wishes of mankind" (*The Future of an Illusion: The Complete Psychological Works of Sigmund Freud*, James Strachey trans. and ed., The Hogarth Press Ltd, 1961, XXI, p. 30). Religion, he believed, was a mental defense against the hardships of life. Threatening aspects of life such as earthquakes, floods, storms, diseases and inevitable death "are forces …[which] rise up against us, majestic, cruel and inexorable" (ibid., p. 16). As such, Man looks for some kind of security through which he is able to escape many of these threatening issues. And if he is not able to, at least he should feel that such disasters have an exalted purpose. This compels the existence of an ultimate "Father Figure," an infinite Being who is able to stop any natural disaster or disease, and in the event that He does not, has proper reason to cause these calamities to occur in the first place. This, claims Freud, is the reason why millions of people, including highly intelligent individuals, believe in God. It is not the result of an intelligent understanding of this world, but "the universal obsessional neurosis of humanity" which would be rejected once people would finally learn to face the world, relying no longer upon illusions but upon scientifically authenticated knowledge.

In *Totem and Taboo*, Freud introduced his famous Oedipus complex. (Oedipus is a famous figure in Greek mythology who unknowingly killed his father and married his mother; the Oedipus complex of Freudian theory is the child's unconscious jealousy of his father and longing for his mother.) Strangely enough, Freud uses this complex to explain the tremendous emotional intensity of religious life and the associated feelings of guilt for failure or obligation to obey the behest of the deity. He postulates a stage of human prehistory in which the family or tribe unit was the "primal horde," consisting of father, mother and offspring. The father as the head of the family or tribe retained exclusive rights over all the females and drove away, or even killed, his sons who challenged his authority. The sons, seeing that they could never challenge their father's authority, consequently decided to kill their father and (being cannibals) consumed him! This, states Freud, is the "primal" crime out of which guilt was born and is responsible for so much tension within the human psyche. (Freud saw the Oedipus complex as universal.) It ultimately developed into moral inhibitions and other phenomena now found in religion since the sons, struck with remorse, could not succeed to their father's position.

This is the reason why the Father Figure, which later developed into the god idea, became so powerful in the human mind and explains why people are religious. It is the result of a deep feeling of guilt and the need to rectify the killing or rejection of this god by way of total obedience.

A great many scholars have discussed and criticized Freud's theory. Clearly, Freud was influenced by Darwin and Robertson Smith, two dominating figures in the nineteenth century, who initiated the "primal horde" theory. Modern anthropologists have rejected this theory. (See H. L. Phillip, *Freud and Religious Belief*, London, Rocklif, 1956.) Freud's Oedipus complex has also come under severe attack, and few contemporary scholars take it seriously.

While Freud considered himself to be an atheist, and seemed to have misunderstood most of religion, this does not mean that he was entirely wrong in his theory that many people are religious because they wish a God to exist to whom they can turn in times of great need. Surprising, however, is the fact that he concluded that *since* Man wishes God to exist, one *must* conclude that His existence is a fantasy. This makes little sense. The fact that Man wishes God to exist has, after all, no bearing at all on the question of whether He really exists or not. He may quite well exist, and simultaneously Man may have a great need for His existence. Nowhere did Freud give any justification for his atheism, but without realizing it, he inadvertently hit upon one of the great foundations of Jewish thought.

Jewish Tradition teaches that Man was created in God's image (*Bereishit* 1:27). Whatever this may mean, it definitely includes the element that God created Man in such a way that, in a desperate search of self-discovery, he would constantly seek God out. Freud, we believe, provided a most original interpretation of this dimension. His discovery of the Father Figure may have uncovered the mechanism through which God created an idea of Himself as the ultimate Father in the human mind. The establishment of the utter dependence of a child on his loving parents may very well have been the model on which God built the foundation for Man's capacity to believe and trust in Him. It would probably not be incorrect to state that according to some rabbinical schools, this was the very reason why God decided in favor of parenthood over other options (such as the creation of human beings without the need for parents—see the creation of Adam and Chava). Rabbinical tradition suggests that God first created the Torah as a primordial substance after which He created the world accordingly. In that case, He may very well have created the need for Man to see God as the great Father Figure, and consequently decided, on a microcosmic level, to create the need for parents.

− 22 −

Human Autonomy and Divine Commandment I

ONE OF THE MOST discussed issues in the world of religious thought today is the question of human autonomy, on the one hand, and Man's obligation to listen and respond to God's commands, on the other. What is the highest religious value: to serve God in a spontaneous outburst of religious devotion (*autonomy*) or to obey and follow the Divine imperative (*obedience*)?

Over the many years, Jewish thinkers have grappled with this issue and tried to provide some kind of solution to this dilemma. No doubt, spontaneity must play a crucial role in the religious experience, but, on the other hand, who will be wise enough to know what makes a spontaneous outburst of religiosity into an *authentic* service of God?

We find several incidents in the Torah where Man actively decided to take religious devotion into his own hands, and paid a heavy price. Well known is the incident where Nadav and Avihu, sons of Aharon, brought strange (or illicit) fire into the Tent of Meeting and lost their lives because of this autonomous act (*Vayikra* 10:1–2). The controversial professor Yeshayahu Leibowitz, *z"l*, relying heavily on earlier commentaries, wrote:

> Just as it is possible for a person to be drawn to regard the [golden] calf as god even when his intention was to worship God [see *Sforno* and *Meshech Chochma* commentaries on the incident], the worship of God itself, if not performed with an awareness that one is obeying an order of God, but because of an inner drive to serve God, is a kind of idolatry—even when

the person's intentions are to serve God. The faith which is expressed in the practical *mitzvot*, in the worship of God, is not something which is meant to give expression or release to man's emotions, but its importance lies in the fact that the person has accepted upon himself, what in the post-biblical tradition is known as, the Yoke of the Kingdom of Heaven and the Yoke of the Torah and *mitzvot*. Faith is expressed in the acts which man does due to his awareness of his obligation to do them, and not because of an internal urge.... [Otherwise,] this is illicit fire.

(*Accepting the Yoke of Heaven*, Urim Publications, 2000, p. 105)

Careful reading of a comment by *Ohr HaChayim* seems to support this view: he wonders why *Parashat Lech Lecha* starts with an unusual introductory phrase: "And God spoke to Avraham: Leave your country...." (*Bereishit* 12:1). This is the first time in the Torah that God speaks to Avraham; surely it would have been more appropriate to use a different phrase: "And God *appeared* to Avraham and said: *Lech Lecha*...." The absence of this phrase, for *Ohr HaChayim*, means that there was Divine speech, but *no* Divine revelation. In other words, there was no exalted religious experience that would have transformed Avraham, but "just" a voice speaking to him, which he automatically recognized as coming from God.

Ohr HaChayim (*Bereishit* 12:1) responds (in his second answer) that this was due to the fact that up until now, Avraham had not yet received any Divine commandment to which he had responded with absolute commitment. "God refused to grant Avraham the ultimate revelation until He put him to the categorical test. And what is this test? *If he will keep His commandments or not.*" Only after Avraham shows that he is fulfilling God's commandments (*obedience*), is He willing to appear to him and have him undergo a religious experience of the highest order. It is for this reason that the commandment of *Lech Lecha* was not prefixed with: "And God *appeared* to Avraham." It is only when Avraham has fulfilled this commandment does the Torah informs us that *now* God actually appears to him (see *Bereishit* 12:7).

As has been suggested, this may provide an answer to a crucial question related to one of the most heroic episodes in Avraham's life, the narrative concerning the "*Kivshan haEsh*" in which Nimrod, the despot of those days, and Avraham's arch enemy, throws him into a furnace to be killed (the first Holocaust experience of the first Jew) after Avraham refuses to stop teaching his fellowman about God. (Nimrod has told him instead to command the people to worship Nimrod himself.) This unprecedented heroism by Avraham is not even mentioned in the text of the Torah (only in the Oral Torah, *Pirkei deRabbi Eliezer*). A possible explanation to this fundamental question may quite well be based on our earlier observations: however impressive this episode may have been, *it in no way sets the standards for Jewish worship*. In this instance, Avraham acts autonomously. This act was *not* commanded; no doubt it was a correct and most desired response towards Nimrod, but nonetheless it was an *autonomous* one. As such, it lacked the fundamental disposition of a religious act of which the Torah was to give evidence. Spontaneity, then, seems only to have value when it **deepens** the *mitzva*, not when it tries to replace it.

Human Autonomy and Divine Commandment II

In our previous thought, we discussed the issue of human autonomy versus Divine commandment. Which is of higher religious value: service of God as an outburst of religious devotion (*autonomy*) or the obligation to obey and to follow the Divine *imperative*? We concluded that it is the Divine *imperative* that turns an act into a religious one. Who, after all, will be wise enough to know what turns a spontaneous outburst of religiosity into an authentic service of God? Faith is expressed in the act which Man performs due to his awareness of his obligation, and *not* because of an internal urge. The most outspoken testimony of this fact is derived from the incident of "illicit fire" which was brought by the sons of Aharon in the Tent of Meeting. Nadav and Avihu paid with their lives when a deeply religious urge overtook their commitment to religious obligation (*Vayikra* 10:1–2). Spontaneity, then, seems only to have value when it *deepens* a *mitzva*, not when it tries to replace it.

However, an incident in the life of Avraham makes us wonder if our earlier observation is indeed tenable. After being informed that his nephew, Lot, was captured by several kings (*Bereishit* 14:12), Avraham organized an army of three hundred and eighteen men and pursued the kings "as far as Dan" (14:14). Fighting these kings was far from easy and highly risky. Only a little earlier, these monarchs had defeated the king of Sodom and Amora. Clearly there was a serious possibility that Avraham's army would be defeated too. From a halachic-ethical point of view, Avraham was not under any obligation to try to save Lot. One does not have to put oneself into a high-risk situation to save another from death.

According to the Talmud (*Avoda Zara* 25a), our patriarchs were called "*Yesharim*," "those who were absolutely straight." Commentators explain that they possessed unusual objectivity and were hardly influenced by external negative forces. In fact, the sages went so far as to claim that the patriarchs did not always behave according to "halachic" standards, but conducted themselves with even higher moral ideals, especially when dealing with their fellowmen. This is so well expressed in the Yiddish, but untranslatable, idiom: "*Menschlichkeit.*"

Ramban explains that Lot had gone out of his way to look after Avraham who was already an old man, and for this reason wandered with him from place to place so as to serve him (19:29). (In fact, this is the reason why Lot came to dwell in Sodom; otherwise he would still have been in Charan.) Consequently, Avraham believed that Lot *had* to be saved when this city in which he lived was to be destroyed, "since it is inconceivable that some evil should overtake him [Lot] because of [the fact that he had looked after] Avraham" (Ramban).

It may be argued that many of the narratives within the book of *Bereishit* reflect this ideology. The great nineteenth-century bible commentator, Rabbi Naftali Zvi Yehuda Berlin, known as the *Netziv*, goes out of his way to emphasize that the patriarchs showed the greatest amount of compassion, *even* towards idolaters. His dramatic words are well taken:

> Besides the fact that they were *tzaddikim* (righteous) and *chassidim* (pious) and showed great love towards God, they were also "*yesharim*," i.e., they behaved respectfully towards the most distasteful idolaters; they [the patriarchs] related to them in a loving way and were concerned about their welfare since this is the foundation of all civilization.... This is clearly to be deduced from the degree to which Avraham struggled and pleaded with God to spare the people of Sodom who were thoroughly wicked...and how Yitzchak went out of his way to appease the shepherds of Avimelech who made him great and awful difficulties.... The same is true about Yaakov who showed infinite tolerance towards his father-in-law, Lavan.
>
> (*Ha'emek Davar*, Introduction to *Bereishit*)

These observations by the *Netziv* are even more surprising once one realizes that the Torah later introduces the law of "*Lo Techanem*"—"You shall not show them [the idolaters] any favor" (*Devarim* 2:2), which has far-reaching halachic import for the relationship between Jews and idol worshipers. It seems, therefore, that this law is of limited application only.

We must therefore conclude that a distinction should be made: in the sphere of the relationship between Man and God, one must conduct his religious life out of a genuine notion of *obligation* and not translate spontaneous urges into self-imposed rituals. In that case, "extra-religious ritualism" is unacceptable. But, when one deals with the proper relationship between Man and his fellowman, a spontaneous act beyond the requirement of the law is encouraged and Man's autonomous input is respected.

— 24 —

Freedom of Will and Determinism
A Daring Midrash

"WE *must* believe in freedom of will, we have no choice." This observation made by Isaac Bashevis Singer introduces one of the greatest problems in Jewish and secular philosophy—the dilemma of freedom of will versus determinism. Many have attempted to solve the issue, but not one philosopher has been able to come up with a completely satisfactory response.

In *Midrash Tanchuma*, we come across one of the most daring statements ever made in religious literature. It is a most telling example of the boldness of our sages, who were not afraid to deal with the problem of freedom of will "head on."

On the words "And Yosef was brought down to Egypt" (*Bereishit* 39:1), the midrash comments: "This is what is referred to when it says in *Tehillim* (66:5): 'Come and see the works of God. He is terrible in His dealing (*allila*) with men.'"

The expression "*allila*" is open to many translations and is unclear. Still, on the surface, this verse in which the word appears seems to express a principal Jewish belief that teaches Man about the greatness of God. Viewed in this light, the translation of "*allila*" seems to convey the concept of awesomeness. However, it is clear that the midrash realizes that the expression, "*allila*," is in fact most unconventional, for it continues with the following words:

Says Rabbi Yehoshua ben Korcha, "Even those events which You [God] bring upon us, You bring with '*allila*.' Before God created the world, He created the Angel of Death on the first day." From where do we know this? Said Rabbi Barchiah, "Because it is written [when the creation had just started]: 'there was darkness upon the face of the deep.' This is a reference to the Angel of Death who darkens the face of all creatures. Man was created on the sixth day and an '*allila*' was placed before him so that he [Man] would bring death upon the world, as it is written, 'And on the day that you will eat from it [i.e., the Tree of Knowledge] you will surely die' (*Bereishit* 2:17)." This means that *from the outset* it was determined that Adam and Eve would be *forced* to eat from the tree, because they *had* to be mortal since God had already created the necessity for death.

It now becomes clear what the word "*allila*" means according to the midrash: *false accusation, pretext* or *insidiousness*. Yet, according to the plain text of the Torah, death came on Man because Man *chose* to eat from the tree.

In case we question the correctness of this interpretation, let us read the continuation of this midrash in which the following analogy is brought:

> To what can we compare this case? To a man who wished to divorce his wife. Before he went home, he wrote a "*get*" (bill of divorce) and entered the house with the "*get*" in his pocket. He then sought an "*allila*" to give it to her. He told her, "Pour me a cup that I may drink." She poured it for him. When he took the cup from her, he said, "Here is your '*get*.'" She said to him, "What did I do wrong?" He said, "Go out of my house because you poured for me a lukewarm cup." Said she to him, "Did you already know that I would pour for you a lukewarm cup, so that you wrote a '*get*' and brought it in your hand?" So Adam said to the Holy One blessed be He, "Lord of the universe, before You created the world, the Torah was with You for 2,000 years [i.e., eternally]. You wrote in the Torah about 'a man who dies in a tent' (*Bamidbar* 19:14), and now you come to accuse me that *I* brought death to the world!!"

The midrash continues in a similar vein, recounting the story of Moshe and the waters of "*meriba*" (the episode in which Moshe sinned by hitting the rock instead of speaking to it as God had instructed him after he has asked for water for the people of Israel [*Bamidbar* 20]). The midrash proves from the text that this sin was already determined long before Moshe erred in this way, and still he was blamed for having brought about his own downfall due to this "transgression."

The third example brought by the midrash relates to Yosef and the exile in Egypt. In *Bereishit* (15:13), we read that Avraham is told by God, "Know for sure that your descendants will be aliens in a land which is not theirs and will be slaves and oppressed for four hundred years." Says the midrash: God blamed the entire affair of Yaakov and his sons, the jealousy and the hatred between the brothers and Yosef, the sale of Yosef, his elevation to high office in Egypt and ultimately the coming of Yaakov and his sons to Egypt, on all of them in order to fulfill what He had said to Avraham.

In other words: the brothers are blamed for having caused all this to happen when, in actual fact, the whole outcome was already decided in advance! Therefore it is an "*allila*" upon Man!

Those who study this narrative very carefully will realize, however, that the midrash was not forced to give this interpretation. It could have allowed for an explanation which would lean towards the concept of freedom of will. Therefore we must conclude that it *deliberately* took this route to emphasize the paradox of freedom of will versus determinism and to teach us an important lesson. When Jews declare, "*Hakol min hashamaim chutz meyirat shamaim*—everything is from Heaven [determinism] except the fear of Heaven [freedom of will]," they pronounce a most profound tenet of Jewish belief. It is not that there are certain times when determinism operates, and other times when freedom of will is given to Man; rather, they function simultaneously. On one level, Man seems to have the opportunity to choose, however, on a different level, all is predetermined. This is one of the great paradoxes of human existence. It reminds us of an observation by Friedrich Durrenmatt who once said that "he who confronts himself with the paradoxical, exposes himself to reality" ("21 Points," The Physicists, 1962).

– 25 –

The Chosen People: An Arrogant Claim?

O NE OF THE MOST disturbing claims ever proffered by any group of people is the one Jews make when, quoting the Bible, they insist upon being called the "Chosen People." For nearly four thousand years, Jews have upheld the belief that they are God's elect, the "apple of His eye," His most beloved and favored nation. This claim belies prejudice of the highest order, branding the vast majority of mankind as second-class citizens.

Aside from biblical references, the Jewish Tradition emphasizes Jewish particularity wherever possible. Jews are not to marry non-Jews. Judaism does not missionize or go out to win converts; rather it discourages all but the most sincere. Laws of *Kashrut* limit social interaction. Even when living amidst their non-Jewish neighbors, Jews have always strived to live in an insulated environment, adopting their own dress code, speaking their own language, and abiding by their own unique customs, prayers and culture. It was the famous English author, George Bernard Shaw, who accused the Jews of arrogance, and said that as long as they insisted upon their chosenness, they had no right to object to the monstrous way in which the Germans had killed six million of their people—they had brought it on themselves. Another English author, H. G. Wells, called the Jewish claim "a hindrance to world unity." Protestant theologians often speak about the "haughtiness of Jewish belief."

Based on the above, it may strike us as paradoxical that traditional Judaism has gone out of its way to stress the dignity of the *entire* human race. In the Creation chapter (long before the Jews come on the scene), the Torah tells us that all mankind are created in the image of God (*Bereishit* 1:27). The prophet's words are clear: "Have we not all one Father? Has not one God created us?" (*Malachi* 2:10). In talmudic times, Rabbi Meir stated that Adam was created from dust that had been collected from all corners of the earth, so that no single nation could claim the distinction of being superior or having cradled mankind. While Judaism does not actively encourage conversion, it does insist that all people *can* become Jews. Some of the greatest Jews in history were converts or descendants of converts: the great King David descends from the lineage of Ruth, perhaps the most famous convert in all history (see the Book of Ruth). Rabbi Akiva, Shemayah, and Avtalyon, some of the greatest sages in the Jewish Tradition, all traced themselves back to converted forefathers. One of the most famous converts was Onkelos, the original biblical commentator and sage, who was born the nephew of the Roman Emperor.

Most surprising is the insistence of the Jewish Tradition to allow even members of the nation of Amalek (see *Shemot* 17), the arch enemy of the Israelites, to convert, once they show a sincere desire to do so (see Rabbi Yechiel Weinberg: *Responsa Sridei Esh*, vol. 2, Mosad HaRav Kook, 1966, p. 104).

The contradiction is obvious: Judaism wants to secure the Jewish people's uniqueness and chosenness, on the one hand, but also wants to uphold the equality and dignity of all human beings, on the other. In fact, it declares that this paradox is the cornerstone upon which all traditional Judaism stands.

Before trying to address this paradox, we must first ask ourselves an important question: Does historical reality confirm the unique status of the Jewish people? The answer is clear: Yes. The cold historical facts prove that the Jewish people are distinct in three matters:

1. They experienced a most miraculous survival.
2. They have made incredible contributions to civilization that are totally out of proportion to their numbers.
3. They made a totally unprecedented return to their homeland after nearly two thousand years of exile.

Throughout history, Jews were surrounded by enemies who were committed to destroying them. They waged war after war in order to survive. They were sent into exile after exile. Beaten, killed, tortured, they were expelled from one country to another, only to find further disaster awaiting them. They became the scapegoat for national and social hysteria. Still, they survived.

Discriminated against, consistently outlawed, the oldest nation on the planet, the Jews, were constantly dying… yet never died. Outlasting all their enemies, they violated all the rules of history, and for this reason they became either the most *irritating* or the most *celebrated* people of the world.

Jews brought monotheism to the world: the most powerful idea Man has ever encountered. Since that day, the universe has never been the same. The gift of the Torah turned all deeds into moral actions, teaching ethics and justice. Neither Christianity nor Islam would exist without the Jews. The world's legal systems are based on "the Book." No international or American law would be what it is today without the Torah. In later centuries, Jews contributed to science, literature, music, finance, medicine and art—all beyond anyone's expectations of a small, tormented people. They were involved in many social revolutions, often becoming the great leaders and thinkers of their generation. They have produced great rabbis and sages, and even those who were on the assimilation road revolutionized the world: Spinoza, Freud, Marx and Einstein.

In 1948, Jews managed to free themselves from their nearly two-thousand-year exile to return to the land of their forefathers. Just moments after they had experienced their worst catastrophe, the Holocaust, in which they lost six million of their fellow Jews, they picked up their bags and "went home." At a time when the whole world declared that there was no longer a future for the Jew, the State of Israel emerged—as if from out of nowhere.

The Jews' return to their homeland is totally unprecedented. No nation after such a long, painful exile has successfully returned to its homeland and, violating all principles of historical conformity, built a modern state.

So Jews are indeed "a nation apart." Their uniqueness is beyond question, but does this have anything to do with the biblical claim of chosenness? To answer this, we must turn to the Torah itself, to *Bereishit* chapter 11. The generation of the Tower of Babel represented a low point in human history. Mankind sought to build a tower high enough to reach the heavens and challenge God. For the first time, a whole generation stood up and rebelled against God as a matter of principle. While earlier generations had done much evil, they recognized their actions as such. The Tower's generation, however, brought a new ideology into the world, one of extreme secularism, in which God was deliberately ignored and in which evil was admired. This new belief system saw nothing wrong with immorality—it elevated it to the new world order.

One man alone understood the inherent dangers of an ideology in which God was exiled and where immorality, corruption, and sexual depravity became the norm. He became known to the world as "Avraham the Ivri" (the Hebrew). By "crossing" (*ivri*), and standing on the "other side," he challenged the world and became the first Jew in history. An eternal moral protestor who taught his fellowman what they did not want to hear but had to know: *It is not what one has which counts but what one is!* It is not what Man *wants* to do, but what he *ought* to do, that transforms him into a being of supreme greatness.

Assisted by Sara his wife, and later by his son Yitzchak and his grandchildren, Avraham built an empire of spiritual ambassadors whose task it was to revolutionize Man's perspective of himself, leading to a better world order. In this way, and not without encountering major stumbling blocks and failures along the way, the "chosen people" came into existence with the specific task of saving and upholding the honor of mankind. The nation that was in the process of being built was to become the guilty conscience of the world. As the French philosopher Jacques Maritain remarked, "The Jews give the world no peace, they bar slumber, they teach the world to be discontented and restless as long as the world has no God."

ও

To be a force of inspiration requires the need to build a powerhouse of spirituality within oneself. It requires a kind of uncompromising dedication towards a common commitment which is only possible through the acceptance of a special way of life. This is Judaism for Jews. To go one's own way means to reject the way of others.

Because Jews live their own distinct lives, and retain their separateness by staying together, they were, and are, able to offer the world an ideology of ultimate value. There is no need for others to live that life as well. It is the intrinsic plurality of Man which offers many faith communities. As long as the ground norms of morality as taught by Avraham are observed, each man or woman has his or her own contribution to make. The exclusiveness of the Jews is therefore of an unusual kind. *National exclusiveness is transformed into ethical exclusiveness. And to abandon national exclusiveness is to abandon the ethical message towards all Man.*

Israel is a world-transforming nation. Its task is to bring mankind back to its full moral and religious potential. In that sense, Jews live in constant spiritual tension. They dream about a *chosen mankind* which has rediscovered its way to God and righteousness. As such, this presents them with a sublime paradox: they struggle to survive with the hope that one day they will be able to disappear.

– 26 –

The Quest for Denial

ONE OF THE MOST common psychological states human beings find themselves in is denial. Each person represses unpleasant experiences and does not want to be confronted with reality when it is not to their liking. Sigmund Freud was the first authority in the secular world to give full attention to this phenomenon. Still, there is plenty of evidence to suggest that this problem was identified even in the earliest moments in human history.

In *Shemot* (14:11–12), we read about a most bizarre complaint against Moshe. After the Israelites had left Egypt, having witnessed the ten plagues and the subsequent downfall of Pharaoh, Moshe is accused by his own people of having brought them into a situation of total disaster. Once they realize that Pharaoh and his army are chasing them, they say:

> Are there no graves in Egypt that you [Moshe] have taken us away to die in the wilderness? What is this that you have done to us, to carry us forth out of Egypt? Is this not the very thing that we told you in Egypt, saying: "Let us be, and we will serve the Egyptians, for it is better for us to serve the Egyptians than to die in the wilderness?"

This is a most remarkable, and seemingly deliberate, rewriting of what had actually taken place. An attitude of "We told you so" is masterfully implemented. Even more surprising is the Jews' attitude after having experienced the unprecedented miracle of the splitting of the Red Sea, as they once more revert to their psychological fabrications:

Then, the whole congregation of the children of Israel murmured against Moshe and Aharon in the wilderness. And the children of Israel said to them: "Oh that we had died by the hand of God in the land of Egypt, while we sat at the fleshpots of Egypt, and we did eat bread to the full, for you have brought us out into the wilderness to make the whole generation die of hunger."

(Shemot 16:2–3)

The whole argument is most astonishing. Was there really a choice between living a life of tranquility in Egypt and dying in the wilderness? Most informative is the fact that God's name is invoked so as to strengthen the argument!

There are several ways to understand this phenomenon of radical self-deception. Obviously, the Israelites were fully aware that their past was definitely not one of tranquility and did not consist of sitting at the fleshpots! We suggest that they did not intend to deny the *past* persecution at the hands of the Egyptians, but that they wanted to deny any *future* problems that could occur if they were to return to Egypt. "Now that Pharaoh has been without us for some time, he surely has realized that we are a great asset to his nation and the future of his government. He is in need of the 'Jewish *kopf*,' the Jewish brain, to run and develop his country. So let us return home in triumph! We shall be received with dignity and prestige. Why are you, Moshe, not allowing us to send word to Pharaoh and say that we are sorry that we left and will return 'home.' No doubt he will have mercy on us and escort us back to Egypt! He has learned his lesson and from now on, we will greatly benefit in the land of Egypt, and live in tranquility and indeed eat from its fleshpots!"

Even after the splitting of the Red Sea, this argument still stands. "God only split the Red Sea to show Pharaoh and the Egyptians what a prestigious people we are and that we therefore should be welcomed with open arms in Egypt and given the most affluent positions in the country. A new world has been opened, and it is time to realize that. And if you, Moshe, ask us how we know that this is exactly what God has in mind, we respond that He would have otherwise given us plenty of food in the desert, and we would not have been chased by Pharaoh! So all that is happening to us is a clear indication that we are 'halachically' obligated to return to Egypt!"

This was only the beginning of a history of grandiose self-deception, ultimately leading to Jewish self-hatred, which, in turn, became the root of animosity against anyone who did not identify with this kind of self-imposed denial of the Jewish cause. "The reason why Pharaoh did all these terrible things to us is because he sensed that we wanted to leave! His astrologers told him that there was a child to be born who would become our redeemer and therefore he started to kill our boys" (Rashi, *Shemot* 1:16). But if we would have stayed, and no such dreams of freedom would have overtaken us, nothing unpleasant would have happened to us! We would have been part of the Egyptian *"cultur gesellschaft"* and everything would have been fine. It is because we have worked with double loyalties that we have had to pay the price.

This may very well have been the reason why Moshe at the Burning Bush refused to respond to God's command to become the redeemer, claiming that he had a speech impediment (*Shemot* 4:10). He did not want to take this task upon himself because he realized that when he would return to Egypt, Jews would say to him: "It all started with you! Because of you, our children were killed! So leave us alone and forget your aspirations to be our redeemer." This would indeed have rendered him speechless.

Looking into Jewish history and at current events, we realize that the above arguments sound all too familiar!

– 27 –

The Mystery of Revelation

IF ANYONE WOULD ever argue that traditional Judaism is guilty of too much dogma, and not enough imaginative thought, a closer look at the plethora of rabbinical insights into the idea of revelation would cure him of such ideas.

When speaking about Moshe's conversation with God in the Tent of Meeting, the Torah says:

> When Moshe entered the Tent of Meeting to speak with Him, he heard the Voice speaking to him from above the cover which is on the ark of testimony, from between the two *cheruvim*, and He spoke to him.
>
> (*Bamidbar* 7:89)

Most remarkable is the fact that the verse twice repeats that God spoke to Moshe: "he heard the Voice speaking to him...and He spoke to him." Looking at the Hebrew, we discover something even more unusual. Based on the *masora*—the traditional way in which the words in the Torah are pronounced (there are no vowels under the Hebrew letters!)—we read, "And he heard the Voice (*midaber*) to him." Would we not have received such a tradition, we would undoubtedly have read "*medaber*," which means "And he heard the Voice speaking to him [i.e., Moshe]." "*Midaber*" is, however, a *hithpael*, a reflexive form of the verb. "*Midaber*," then, reflects back to the one who is speaking, i.e., God. In that case, the translation should be: "And he [Moshe] heard the Voice speaking to Him [i.e., God Himself]."

Thus Rashi comments: "This is an expression similar to '*mitdaber*' [reflexive]. He spoke between Him and Himself, and Moshe heard." In other words, God was really in conversation with Himself and Moshe "overheard" this. This caused Moshe to have an inner acoustic experience in which, according to Rashi's bold words, he heard God speak to Himself. It is in this way that God "spoke" to Moshe.

This observation is very close to Maimonides' understanding of prophecy, as explained in several parts of his famous *Guide for the Perplexed*. For those who are familiar with Maimonides' general philosophical approach, this insight comes as no great surprise, but for Rashi, who is not known for his philosophical speculations, it is all the more unique. We must therefore conclude that this observation is not just the manifestation of philosophical inquiry but a basic foundation of Jewish belief. Still, most commentators do not pause at this fact, and the translations of the *targumim* (Onkelos and Yehonatan) make no distinction between "*medaber*" and "*midaber*."

Many years after Rashi, the great Italian sixteenth-century commentator, Rabbi Ovadia Sforno, seems to relate to Rashi's observation. In one of his most profound statements, he comments on our verse as follows:

> "*Midaber elav*": Between Him and Himself, for "God does everything for Himself" (*Mishlei* 16:4), and by knowing Himself, He knows and does good to others, and the action manifests itself to the one affected by God in accordance with his capacity, and so it is true about every case in the Torah where it says, "And God spoke."

As is apparent in many other cases, Jewish commentators struggle with the notion of revelation. All agree that revelation *did* occur as told by the Torah, but, since the text is silent about the "how," the sages and later rabbinic thinkers showed unusual creativity when dealing with the nature of this Divine disclosure.

Johann Sebastian Bach,
Spinoza and *Halacha*

ARNOLD TOYNBEE, the great, though mildly anti-Semitic, historian of the last century, is quoted as saying that "history is the tragedy of what could otherwise have been." When contemplating this comment, we wonder what would have happened if Johann Sebastian Bach, genius musician and composer, would have crossed paths with Benedictus (Baruch) Spinoza, world-renowned philosopher, a Jew by birth, and foremost critic of Judaism.

It is our thesis that in a meeting between these two great minds, Bach would have staunchly defended the world of *Halacha*, while Spinoza would have informed Bach that he did not appreciate his music as much as he did Beethoven's. This may sound ludicrous. Bach, after all, was a most devout Christian. He was a Lutheran, and it may be argued that Lutheranism is further away from Judaism than any other Christian denomination. And what has Spinoza in common with Beethoven, who lived long after he did?

Spinoza is famous for his rejection of Jewish Law. To him, Judaism and, even more so, *Halacha* is a kind of religious behaviorism, in which outward action is idolized and inner devotion is of secondary importance. Judaism, according to Spinoza, is a well-organized discipline, in which tradition and careful observance have the upper hand. To obey and to follow all the minutiae of the Law is the ultimate goal of the religious Jew. There is "no place for lofty speculations nor philosophical reasoning. I would be surprised if I found [the prophets] teaching any new speculative doctrine, which was not commonplace to... gentile philosophers." He believed that for Judaism, "the rule of right living, the worship and the love for God was to them rather a bondage than the true liberty, the gift and grace of the Deity" (Tractatus Theologico Politicus III, XIII).

Spinoza's main objection against Jewish Law is its confinement of the human spirit and its intellectual constraint. It does not allow for any novelty or intellectual creativity. All that the rabbis did, as they developed biblical law, was to spin a web, so intertwined that it killed its very spirit, turning the religious Jew into a robot. As such, the Jew became a slave to the law and the law became a yoke. (It is not surprising that many gentile philosophers echoed Spinoza's critique: Emanuel Kant and Hegel maintained that Judaism is "eigentlich gar keine Religion" [actually not a religion].)

Indeed, this seems to be a bitter critique on the foundations of Judaism, and is not to be easily defeated. What then should be our response?

Those who carefully explore the music of Johann Sebastian Bach will be surprised to discover that the great musician dealt with music as the rabbis dealt with the law. He was totally traditional in his approach to it, adhering strictly to the rules of composing music, as understood in his days. Nowhere in all his compositions do we find deviation from these rules. But what is most surprising is that Bach's musical output is not only unprecedented but, above all, astonishingly creative. According to many, he was the greatest composer of all times. Anybody with a sound background in music, after carefully listening to his St. Matthew Passion, will admit that this is probably the most beautiful composition ever written within the Western tradition of classical music. (This is not simply the private observation of a rabbi, but an opinion stated by several outstanding music critics!) What we discover is that the self-imposed restrictions of Bach, to conform to the traditional rules of composition, molded him into a composer of such outstandingly creative music that nobody after him was ever able to follow in his footsteps. It was from within the "confinement of the law" that Bach burst out with unprecedented creativity. This proves, against all expectations, that the "finiteness" of the law could lead to infinite riches. What Bach proved, as nobody else could, was that *it is not through novelty that one reaches the deepest of all human creative experiences, but in the capacity to plumb the depths of what is already given.* Bach's works were entirely free of any innovation, yet utterly original.

We do not find this type of conventional creativity in Beethoven's music, who, in his later years, broke with many, although not all, of the accepted rules of composition. He was one of the pioneers of a whole new world of musical options. Certainly his music is of outstanding beauty. But it was his rejection of some of the conventional laws of music which made him *less* of a musical genius. To work within constraints, and *then* to be utterly novel, is the ultimate sign of unprecedented greatness.

This is what Johann Wolfgang Goethe, the great German poet and philosopher, meant when he said:

> In der Beschraenkung zeigt sich erst der Meister,
> Und das Gesetz nur kann uns Freiheit geben.
>
> (Sonnet: "Was wir bringen")

> In limitation does the master really prove himself
> And it is [only] the law which can provide us with freedom.

Bach, then, was a "halachic" giant of the first order. He realized the falsehood behind the belief that when one adopts a well-defined scheme, one forfeits an inner life experience of great spiritual profundity.

This is indeed why we maintain that Spinoza would have preferred Beethoven over Bach. What Spinoza did not comprehend when he criticized Jewish law was that restrictive rules, when deeply studied and contemplated, become the impetus of a special kind of infinite creativity, never to be found by those who rejected these very limitations.

It is as if Bach thought that *Halacha* is both a discipline and an inspiration, an act of obedience and an experience of joy, a yoke and a prerogative. Man needs to hear more than he understands in order for him to be able to understand more than he hears.

Any student of Jewish law can no doubt testify that the study of *Halacha*, and leading a life according to its teachings, is one of the most creative of all human endeavors. In the same way that music cannot be played without a musical instrument, no "real" religious Jew can play his soul music without a most sensitive musical instrument called *Halacha*. In fact, it is a recipe for a life of happiness and tranquility.

It is indeed a great tragedy that Spinoza was not able to meet Bach. If he would have, he may have become an even greater philosopher.

v. Holidays and Customs

− 29 −

Mitzvot, Minhagim and Their Dangers

Every morning, a Jewish male is required to cover himself with a *tallit*, a "prayer shawl" which has at its four corners long *tzitzit* (threads), in which certain religious symbols are represented (see *Bamidbar* 15:37–39). (This *tallit* should cover the entire upper body and not just be used as a shawl around one's neck.) The correct way to don this *tallit* is first to cover one's head with it, while keeping the face uncovered. Next, one takes the corners of the garment and throws them over the left shoulder. A common practice is to throw these corners with some force so as to make sure that they will indeed reach the back of the human body. Obviously, this should be done with care, making sure the person standing behind does not get hit by your *tzitzit* in his face or eyes. Unfortunately, this happens all too often in synagogues. At such a moment, a religious tragedy takes place of which many worshipers do not seem to be aware. In their attempt to fulfill a *mitzva*, they are, in actual fact, transgressing the law of being concerned about the welfare of one's neighbor.

On other occasions, we find worshipers running to kiss the Scroll of the Torah when it is removed from the *Hechal* (*Aron HaKodesh*, synagogue ark). In order to get there as fast as possible, or to make sure they will get close enough to be able to kiss it, they often push people aside or step on their feet. It would have been better if they had stayed where they were.

The Talmud calls such an act a "*mitzva haba be'avera,*" fulfilling "a commandment which comes with a transgression." In such a case, the *mitzva* has turned into an irreligious act and has lost all meaning.

One of the *minhagim* observed by the Ashkenazi community before *Yom Kippur* is the custom to "*shlog kappores.*" This is a custom mentioned by

Rema, one of the most important commentators on the *Shulchan Aruch* of Rabbi Yosef Karo, and regarded as the main and decisive authority for Ashkenazi Jewry (see *Shulchan Aruch, Orach Chaim* 7). The *minhag* of "*kappores shloggen*" is to take a live chicken and wave it around one's head as a kind of symbolic atonement for one's sins throughout the previous year. (It is reminiscent of the atonement sacrifices in the Temple, although definitely not a replacement of these sacrifices.) The obvious intent of the Codex is to do this very carefully so that the chicken does not get hurt or scared. There is, after all, a law which states that it is absolutely forbidden to cause any unnecessary pain to an animal or any other creature; this prohibition is called *tza'ar ba'ale chayim*.

Not uncommon is the sight of people, in their eagerness to fulfill this custom, picking up the chicken and mercilessly waving it around, scaring the chicken and often hurting it. Sometimes the chickens are kept in small plastic boxes, within a confined space, without adequate food or water. One wonders how these people can enter *Yom Kippur* in the right frame of mind. They seem to convince themselves that this *mitzva* will earn them even more merit in the eyes of the Almighty. We wonder if this does not invoke rather a different response from the Heavenly Court.

Perhaps it is time that kosher consumers should no longer just look for "*glatt kosher*"* supervision, but also for "*mercy glatt.*" Too many animals are raised in inhumane conditions. While it will be difficult to change these conditions, and meat may become more expensive, rabbinical authorities should consider this possibility. Consumption of Kosher meat, coming from animals who are raised in these inhumane conditions, is, in the eyes of the Jewish Law, a contradiction in terms.

When asked if he was a vegetarian for health reasons, Isaac Bashevis Singer replied, "Yes, for the chicken's health."

---

* The term "*glatt kosher*" originally referred to certain stringent rules relating to *Kashrut* of meat, mainly observed by *Sephardim*. Nowadays, the term encompasses many other stringencies which relate to other Kosher food as well.

Chumrot–Religious Stringencies
Good or Bad?

SELF-IMPOSED SEVERITIES have become part and parcel of the religious Jewish community of today. Many people feel the need to express their religious devotion to God through the acceptance of stringencies which conventional Jewish Law does not in actual fact require. They observe Shabbat more strictly; they make sure that they only eat *glatt kosher*; they use the largest measurements for their *kiddush* cup or, in the case of some married women, cover their hair not once, but twice.

No doubt, there is room for stringencies within Jewish Law. It may even be argued that it would be healthy and prudent if every human being would have his or her specific *mitzva* to which they would devote extra attention. In earlier days, the Torah introduced the "*Nazir*" law, which states that a person who feels the need to deny himself certain pleasures is permitted, and even encouraged, to do so (see *Bamidbar* 6). Sometimes people have to sort out their religious priorities, and they feel that they can only achieve this goal when they abstain from certain liberties, the practice of which would tempt them beyond the border of the permissible.

What many religious people today seem to forget is that striking the right balance will not be achieved by excessive forms of abstinence, but by modest behavioral changes accompanied by some measure of slight discomfort. The Torah suggests, in the case of the *Nazir*, abstinence from certain alcoholic drinks, leaving the hair untrimmed and the beard unshaved. Nothing more. According to talmudic tradition (*Talmud Yerushalmi, Nazir* chapter 1, *Halacha* 3), this should not last longer than 30 days. It warns that longer periods of abstinence will be counterproductive.

Most interesting is the fact that at the end of this thirty-day period, a sin offering has to be brought by the very person who took these stringencies upon himself. Besides this, when the period is over, the Nazirite is *commanded* to drink wine. *This means that the abstinence from permitted pleasures requires atonement because such stringencies are, in fact, and under normal circumstances, prohibited.* The only reason why such restrictions are permitted for short periods is that they will result in the possibility of enjoying these pleasures at a later stage, in a way which is part of one's religious experience, i.e., as a human being who is able to enjoy the gifts of the Almighty. And this is the reason why the Nazirite is told to drink wine. He must, after his period of abstinence, be able to drink wine in the proper, elevated way. It is not the abstinence from wine and other alcoholic drinks which is a major achievement, but the art of enjoying them in the right spirit and with the correct intentions. This is a much greater achievement.

It should be made clear that this is only true when the Torah permits the use of these delights. Drug abuse would not be considered permitted pleasures, since use of drugs may lead to a kind of addiction from which few, if any, are able to free themselves. They are detrimental to the mental and physical health of the human being. Ultimately they destroy the capacity to enjoy life in the higher sense of the word.

Still, sometimes certain stringencies are nothing less than a form of escape a mechanism for self-deception. They are used to hide a lack of proper observance in other religious matters and are often used to cloak unethical behavior. When people misbehave in their relationship with their fellowman, but hide behind their insistence on *glatt kosher* food, we face a deliberate and vulgar misuse of the concept of *chumrot.* (Asking for *glatt kosher* food while sitting in jail for having committed a criminal offence is tantamount to asking, after one has murdered both parents, for dispensation on the grounds that one is an orphan.)

The Talmud (*Baba Kama* 59b) recounts the story of a scholar by the name of Eliezer Ze'era who wore "black shoes" (uncommon in those days) as a sign of mourning for the destruction of Jerusalem. The sages considered this an act of arrogance. They felt that he was trying to show off, so they put him in jail!

On another occasion, the sages opposed a "very religious" person who refused to follow a lenient ruling which they had decided on and nearly excommunicated him (*Baba Kama* 80b).

A story has been told that a rabbi once came to see the famous Jerusalem sage and halachic authority, Rabbi Shlomo Zalman Auerbach, *z"l*. He asked him if a certain *chumra* that was practiced in his community had any foundation in *Halacha*, or simply belonged to the world of religious fancy. The sage responded that there was no foundation for such a stringency and advised the rabbi to tell his community to repeal this practice. Several weeks later, the Jerusalem sage met the rabbi and asked him if he had told his community to stop practicing this mistaken *chumra*. The rabbi turned to the sage and said half-jokingly, "No, it is a leniency which my congregation cannot live with…."

– 31 –

Rosh Hashana and The Day After

THE TORAH READING of the second day of *Rosh Hashana* relates the famous story of *Akeidat Yitzchak* (the offering of Yitzchak by Avraham). Many explanations have been provided as to why this portion should be read on *Rosh Hashana*. (For an overview see: *Sefer HaToda'ah* by Rabbi Eliyahu Kitov. English translation: *The Book of Our Heritage*, Feldheim, NY, 1988, vol. 1, pp. 30–33.) There remains, however, a problem. We would expect that the reading on *Rosh Hashana* would conclude with the final part of this dramatic story which contains also a beautiful Divine promise which is so much in the spirit of the universality of this festival:

> And in your [Avraham's] seed shall all the nations of the earth be blessed.
>
> (*Bereishit* 22:18)

Instead, the synagogue reading continues with a story which is most unusual and even irrelevant for *Rosh Hashana*:

> And it came to pass after these events that information was given to Avraham, saying: "See, Milcah, she, too, has born children unto your brother, Nachor: Utz, his firstborn, and Buz, his brother, and Kemuel, the father of Aram. And Chesed and Hazo and Pildosh and Yidlap and Bethuel. And Bethuel begat Rivka...."
>
> (*Bereishit* 23:20–24)

These verses appear to be of little importance. What message are they trying to convey and why should they be part of the *Rosh Hashana* reading?

Rabbi Joseph B. Soloveitchik *z"l*, of Boston, is known to have commented that the sages may have included this story in the *Rosh Hashana* reading as a warning to all those who attend the synagogue prayers on the High Holidays. In his opinion, this portion is included so as to draw attention to the fact that once the *Akeida* episode had come to an end, "nothing had changed," and that commonplace life just continued as normal. By rights, an event such as the *Akeida* should have caused the world to shake at its foundations. It should have motivated all those who heard about it to better their ways and start a new chapter, but nothing like that actually happened. Once back home, Avraham was not questioned by his neighbors about this episode, nor were they interested in how it affected his personality, or what could be learned from such a shattering experience.

Instead, he encountered a world which was immune to religious experiences, with nothing to say other than that another few children were born; a world of religious irrelevance in which nothing else counted but day-to-day family affairs. One of the greatest moments in Man's history was, as such, trivialized into a spiritual nothingness.

This, Rabbi Soloveitchik warns, is the danger that awaits us all after *Rosh Hashana*. While we may be elevated to the highest level of spiritual exaltation on the day itself, we are warned that on "the morning after," we return back to our former lives without having changed an iota. Instead of asking ourselves and our fellowmen what meaning *Rosh Hashana* had for us, many of us discuss the cantorial excellence (or failure) of the *chazan* or the *ba'al tokea's* wonderful expertise (or failure) as a trumpeter. Similar expressions are common after *Yom Kippur* has ended. One question, possibly the most frequently posed, is, "Did you fast well?" If one would ask somebody to what extent he was *effected* by the *Yom Kippur* prayers, one would be seen as an iconoclast who has lost his religious balance.

We would, however, like to offer another approach, one which would emphasize the other side of the same coin. Perhaps the Torah reading on *Rosh Hashana* continues with the day-to-day affairs of Avraham's family so as to inform us that after Avraham's *Akeida* experience (which transported him to other worlds and transformed his personality in a most drastic way), he did not lose the ground under his feet. He remained a family man, dealing with the often petty trivialities that life brings. He does not cocoon himself in a spiritual oasis, but rather actively participates in all human affairs. Neither does he become absentminded, but stays alert to all mundane matters. This also may be the message which we need to hear after an elevated *Rosh Hashana* experience. Even when we have been (hopefully) transformed by its holiness, we should not try to escape our daily duties and interests in our surroundings. The greatness of Avraham was that even after the experience of the *Akeida*, his family was able to approach him and tell him that "Milcah too has born children."

Rosh Hashana and the Cities of Refuge

O NE OF THE CHALLENGES *Rosh Hashana* and *Yom Kippur* present us with is an awakening to our human vulnerabilities and the difficulties we encounter in overcoming our weaknesses. Every year we take it upon ourselves to defeat our selfish inclinations, to start a new chapter and to accomplish, once and for all, complete *teshuva*. But every year again, we realize, especially in the days immediately preceding the High Holidays, that once more we did not really accomplish this task last year and that our *mitzva* of repentance did not bear too much fruit. We may have started on our journey in fulfilling the great *mitzva* of repentance, but we never completed the mission. This awareness induces mounting frustration and often strong feelings of guilt. It is for that reason that many of us wonder why we should attempt once more to accomplish the great dream of complete *teshuva* when we are more than aware of the fact that, once again, we are sure to fall short in the coming year. What is the point in starting a *mitzva* when there is little chance that one will complete it? At the end of the long journey through the desert, Moshe repeatedly warns his people of the enormous ramifications of not following the ways of the Torah. During lengthy and heavy discourses, in which he reprimands his beloved people for their mistakes, the Israelites enter the Transjordanian territory. Immediately the Torah informs us of Moshe's next deed:

> *Then* Moshe separated three cities on the other side of the Jordan towards the sunrise.
>
> (*Devarim* 4:41)

These are the cities of refuge where the unintentional murderer could flee to after he had accidentally murdered a fellowman (see *Bamidbar* 35). The commentators struggle with this verse, since it is difficult to see the textual context in which it is placed. Why should Moshe, in the middle of his ethical discourses, suddenly introduce the *mitzva* of separating these cities of refuge, especially since he immediately resumes his discourse afterwards? Could not the appointment of these cities have waited until after he finished his ethical discourses? This question is even more pertinent in light of the fact that these three cities would not even function as cities of refuge until another three cities in the land of Israel proper would be dedicated for the same purpose as well! Only after the land was completely inhabited would these six cities be activated as cities of refuge (*Makkot* 9b).

As is well known, Moshe *Rabbeinu* was not allowed to enter the land of Israel. After leading the Jewish people for nearly forty years through the desert, and anticipating the moment he would be able to enter the Promised Land, one incident brings an abrupt halt to his dream. Instead of speaking to the rock to give water to the people of Israel, as God has commanded him, he hits it with his staff. As a result, God tells him that the *mitzva* to live in the land will be withheld from him. Even after pleading with God on several occasions, there is no favorable Divine response and Moshe is asked to no longer appeal for dispensation (see *Bamidbar* 20). This confronts Moshe with some major issues in his religious commitment. Now that he is unable to complete the commandment of appointing *all* six cities of refuge in the land, what is the point in starting this *mitzva*?

Nevertheless, Moshe separates these three cities at the *earliest opportunity*, i.e., when he and the Israelites find themselves at the very site of these cities in Transjordan.

His point is clear and holds great meaning: *one does not postpone or completely ignore a mitzva because one is unsure whether one will ever be able to work for or see its completion.* On the contrary, one should start to fulfill a *mitzva* regardless of the outcome or the extent of its fulfillment. The reason is obvious: even when one does not complete a *mitzva*, there is still a great value in starting it. Every step in the direction of completion is a major achievement. And even when, in the end, all that was achieved seems to have been lost, the value of *trying* to accomplish the *mitzva* has a major impact on the human soul. It is true that the *Yamim Noraim*, the Days of Awe, often make us wonder why we should try to do *teshuva* once more, in the knowledge that there is a considerable chance that we will not make it this year either. Moshe's example, however, shines out: one starts a *mitzva* even when one is not sure that one will complete it. This is even more true when we realize that Moshe knew *without any doubt* that he would never be permitted to complete the *mitzva* of the cities of refuge. We, on the other hand, do not have this absolute certainty of failure of completion. Despite last year's experience, we clearly do have the possibility of completing the *mitzva* of *teshuva* this year. And for those who will not succeed, they should not forget that real religious life is not the level at which one finds oneself spiritually, but how hard one tries to get there! This is clearly alluded to by Rabbi Yosef Karo in his magnum opus, *Shulchan Aruch*, the codex of Jewish law, which starts with the following words: "One should make a supreme *effort* to get up early in the morning like a lion...."

– 33 –

Yom Kippur: A Day Like *Purim**

The *"Ba'alei HaKabbalah"* (kabbalists) discovered mystical associations between *Purim* and *Yom Kippurim*—the only difference in Hebrew spelling between the two names being an initial Hebrew letter *kaf* in the word *Ki-purim. Yom Kippurim,* then, would signify "a day like *Purim.*" This is no doubt a strange association. To suggest that *Yom Kippur* is like *Purim* is a most unusual way of looking at this awesome day. What is the possible meaning behind this observation?

The Talmud in *Shabbat* (88a), in its discussion of the revelation at Sinai, draws our attention to a theological problem. As is commonly known, our forefathers have always been praised for their spontaneous outburst at Sinai when they declared that they would observe the *mitzvot* even before they had an understanding of what was involved. Their proclamation of *"Na'aseh"* (we shall do) before *"Nishma"* (we shall listen) (*Shemot* 24:7) has been viewed as one of the highest levels of religious devotion. Still, our talmudic passage draws our attention to the fact that this devotion was in no way as great as the one which the Jews achieved in the days of *Purim.*

Towards the end of the Book of Esther, we are told that after their miraculous deliverance from the "final solution," masterminded by Haman and devised by the architects of the Persian genocide program, the Jews accepted upon themselves the observance of *Purim* forever after: *"Kiymu ve'kiblu,"* "the Jews confirmed and took on themselves," and their children after them, the

---

* This article was partially inspired by Norman Lamm's, "Neither Here Nor There," *The Royal Reach* (NY: Feldheim, 1970), ch. 2.

obligation to observe these two days of *Purim* (*Esther* 9:27). Logic would dictate here as well that the two key words should be in the reverse order. First they should have "taken" (*kiblu*) this day of *Purim* upon themselves, and then they should have "confirmed" (*kiymu*) it by actually observing *Purim*. It is probably because of this inversion of the proper order in the verse that our rabbis interpret a special meaning in this phrase.

When God revealed his Torah at Sinai, the sages tell us, He lifted up the mountain and held it over the heads of the Israelites, gathered below, as if it were a cask, and said to them, "If you accept the Torah, all well and good; but if not, I shall drop the mountain on your heads and there shall be your burial place." The sages then draw the conclusion that the Israelites were *coerced* into accepting the Torah. In fact, Rabbi Aha ben Yaakov argued that if this is the case then "*moda raba l'oraita*"—this becomes a strong protest against the obligatory nature of the Torah. It is giving notice to God that although He sees the Torah as a permanently binding contract between Himself and Israel, this is far from obvious since a contract signed under duress is invalid! In that case, the Jewish people could argue that it was not really bound by the Torah's requirements! *Rava* highlights, however, that the Israelites reaffirmed the Torah *voluntarily* on the days which *Purim* commemorates. This is the meaning of the words—"*kiymu ve'kiblu*," i.e., that the Israelites *confirmed* and then *accepted*, as explained by the words: "*kiymu mah she'kiblu kevar*." [After the *Purim* incident the Israelites] "confirmed what they long ago had accepted [at Sinai]." So after their deliverance from Haman, the Jews confirmed their voluntary acceptance of the Torah which they were initially forced to accept at Sinai.

There lies a deep theological and psychological insight behind this unusual talmudic passage. A moral act is only authentic when it is issued out of genuine freedom of choice. The Torah is only meaningful when the human being is free in accepting it.

> I have set before you this day life and good and death and evil...and you shall *choose* life.
>
> (*Devarim* 30:15–19)

According to Jewish law, a person cannot be held responsible for an act which he was forced to do. In such a case, a person acted under compulsion and is therefore not liable. This can be seen when one is forced to do a sin, or transgresses a prohibition such as a criminal act performed in a seizure of insanity, or some other form of mental distress. In the same way, one who has performed a *mitzva*, but has done so because of external force, cannot claim credit for performing this good deed. After all, one was forced into this *mitzva*.

This was indeed the problem at the time of the theophany at the top of Sinai. The Israelites had no choice but to accept the Torah. This full confrontation with God had indeed elevated them to such an extent that they were totally robbed of their freedom of will. Clearly this is the meaning of the statement of the sages that "God held the mountain over them." They had no choice but to accept it.

What all this means is that Man's freedom of choice is only exercised when he is not forced to commit a wrongdoing, or, conversely, is not overwhelmed by an unprecedented religious experience. Compulsion and freedom are mutually exclusive. So, where, then, is Man's freedom to be found? In a "neither here nor there" condition. Only when a person is not forced one way or the other. When things are normal, and the world runs its course, and God is neither too much here nor too much absent, only then is Man able to use his freedom of choice.

It is the *Purim* story which embodies this very principle. In those days, there were no *open* miracles which would reveal God to such an extent that the Jews would have lost their freedom to choose. Neither was it a time when God was totally *absent*, which would give cause for the denial of His existence. The victory of the Jews over Haman, and the frustration of his nefarious plot, was a triumph which nobody had really expected nor completely denied. It is only under such conditions that people can make active choices. Hence, if—as they did—they turned to God and accepted the Torah, this signified a genuine and binding commitment, "*kiymu ve'kiblu*"; they confirmed what they had previously agreed on and took it upon themselves.

Based on this, we can begin to understand the reason behind the sages' belief that *Yom Kippurim* is "a day like *Purim*." *Yom Kippur* only has the meaning of a day of atonement when a person lives in *Purim*-like conditions. Only in a situation where God's Providence is not overly revealed, nor too inconspicuous, can Man claim merit for his good deeds. Any other situation would make *Yom Kippur* impossible. If our last year would have consisted of a succession of open miracles, we would have been forced to live a life of righteousness. When, alas, the miracles would abate, we would be left with an overwhelming feeling that God had abandoned us altogether—and that the world has no purpose—resulting in Man regulating his own moral standards, rendering *Yom Kippur* a farce. Only in a case such as *Purim* is Man able to confront his responsibilities in a balanced way. It is for this reason that *Yom Kippurim* is a day **like** *Purim*.

34

Yom Kippur and Arthur Schopenhauer

All religions and philosophies are, without a doubt, confronted with the question of how to relate to "existence." Should one oppose "existence" and ideally opt for "non-existence," or should one see "being" as good and "non-being" as the opposite?

Arthur Schopenhauer, an important nineteenth-century German philosopher, and author of *The World as Will and Idea*, could perhaps be regarded as Europe's greatest pessimist. In his works, Schopenhauer does not have one good word to say in favor of "existence." From his youngest days, he viewed the world as an ongoing disaster, and lived in constant fear that things would only deteriorate. Danger is rampant, and therefore he decided to sleep with a weapon under his pillow and refused to have the barber shave him with a knife, lest he cut his throat. The only one he trusts is his dog, but as for Man, there is no one to have faith in. Life is an ongoing deceit, harsh and cruel.

Why, then, are there optimists in this world? How, then, is it that some people live in joy and see everything in a sanguine light? How is it that these people deny the truth and ignore the fact that this life is really a catastrophe? Why will they not see the truth?

Well, argues Schopenhauer, the aggressively optimistic philosophers of the Western world have fallen prey to a vulgar buoyancy which is rooted in the Jewish Tradition! Jewish traditional optimism reflects "a self-congratulatory human egoism, which is blind to all except our [own] all too frail human goals and aspirations" (*Works*, R. B. Haldane and J Kemp trans., London, Kegan Paul, Trench: Trubner and Co., 1909, vol. III, pp. 305*ff*, 446*ff*). Yes, believe it or not, Jews are guilty of bringing some optimism into the world.

Is it indeed true that Judaism is blind to the tragic? Nobody can deny that Judaism adopts an optimistic view of life, but is this optimism vulgar and self-destructive, and, are we unable, as a result of this shortsightedness, to cope in the face of disaster?

> Rabbi Shimon said: "In the hour that God was about to create Adam, the angels of service were divided. Some said: 'Let him not be created.' Others said, 'Let him be created.' Love said, 'Let him be created, for he will do loving deeds.' But, Truth said, 'Let him not be created, for he will be all falsity.' Righteousness said, 'Let him be created, for he will do righteous deeds.' Peace said, 'Let him not be created, because he will be full of strife.' What, then, did the Holy One Blessed be He do? He seized hold of the truth and cast it to the earth [where it broke into pieces], as it says, 'You cast truth to the ground.' (*Doniel* 8:12)"
>
> (*Bereishit Rabbah* 18.5)

Virtually no midrash should be taken *literally*. Every midrash, however, should be taken *seriously*. When it speaks about the origin of Man, it is trying to give us insight into the human condition. No doubt this is true about this midrash as well. It is, however, clearly "disturbing" because it makes the point that "truth needs to be thrown to the ground" before the creation of Man can take place. It appears that not even God can create Man unless there is a compromise made in which truth pays the price. There is no "all is well" attitude when Man comes on the scene. To create Man, one has to remove all romantically "optimistic" views about human existence. Not even the good Lord, so to speak, has the power to indiscriminately silence all opposition: to create Man is to take a risk, and the pessimists have a point. *Meshech Chochma* (*Bereishit* 1:31) explains that while all creatures were blessed with the pronouncement: "And God saw that it was good," this is not so with Man. Not even God could "see" (in anthropomorphic terms) what Man will become, whether he will be good or bad. For God to "see," says *Meshech Chochma*, implies determinism, i.e., that all creatures will follow their unchanging nature.

Only Man is endowed with free will. He is the great unknown, and hence, the absolute truth, reflected in the existence of God, will have to be compromised, since Man's very purpose is to be a free agent with the ability to deny or ignore God. And so pessimism is born. Man may go wrong and indeed he may become a "Schopenhauer disaster." The midrash knows that truth is cast to the ground, and so all devout Jews know that truth is difficult to bear. But what is the effect of this knowledge? Can it be anything other than despair, as Schopenhauer would have it? There is only one possible response. It is as if the aforementioned midrash has anticipated Schopenhauer: "Then the angels of service said to God, 'Lord of the Universe, how can Thou despise Your seal [the truth]?' And God responded, 'Let Truth arise from the earth, as it says: "Truth springs from the earth."' (*Tehillim* 85:12)"

Certainly, the truth will have to rise from the earth in "broken pieces," but there is a purpose: so that Man will be able to labor to rediscover it, fragment by fragment, without ever seeing the full picture. The truth will not be truth for Man unless he *discovers* it by way of his own effort. Paradoxically, it is Man's potential to stray that creates a realistic optimism; the Jew clings to life, despite Schopenhauer, because he knows that since God was prepared to cast the truth to the ground, there must be a Divine plan beyond Man's comprehension. That is the foundation of balanced optimism as taught by Jewish Tradition.

This, then, is the underlying motive of *Yom Kippur*. It is a protest against Schopenhauer and all dedicated pessimists. It bears testimony and is a warning not to yield to total pessimism as long as the truth springs from the ground. It is an admonition to endure truth and to choose life. *Yom Kippur*, more than any other day of the Jewish year, would seem to carry the seed for Schopenhauer's approach. Yet aside from being a most serious day of fasting, *Yom Kippur* is a festival of joyous life; it is a plea to endure, for it is only defiant endurance which reveals the fact that truth, however broken, remains the seal of God: "*Avinu Malkenu*, seal us in the book of life."

35

Sukkot: Twin Towers and the Paradox of Life

W HEN CONTEMPLATING the festival of *Sukkot*, we are confronted with a remarkable paradox. As is well known, the *sukka* symbolizes our life-span in the world. For what is a *sukka*? It is a frail structure in which we need to dwell for seven days. Many commentators remind us that these seven days represent Man's average life-span, which is about seventy years. This was well stated by King David when he wrote: "The span of his years are seventy and with strength eighty years" (*Tehillim* 90:10). Indeed, under favorable circumstances, we may prolong our stay in this world into our eighth day which is symbolized by *Shemini Chag Atzeret* (a separate festival immediately following the seven days of *Sukkot*).

Indeed how frail our life is! Not only short, but also most unreliable. As long as we live under favorable and healthy circumstances, life is a pleasant experience, and just like the *sukka*, it seems to protect us and we feel safe. But once life begins to unravel serious problems, or seems to turn against us, we realize how little protection it really can offer, and how unstable our existence truthfully is. Like the *sukka*, life is far less secure than we had imagined.

Perplexing, however, is the fact that the festival of *Sukkot* is considered to be the highlight of joy and happiness. Speaking specifically about *Sukkot*, the Torah states: "And you shall be happy on your festival" (*Devarim* 16:14). This means that we should experience the most exalted form of happiness at a time when we have to dwell in a structure which is far from being secure!

In fact, Jewish law makes it abundantly clear that the *sukka* must be built in such a way that it is not able to stand up against a strong wind, that its roof must be leaking when it starts to rain, and that it must contain more shadow than sunlight.

These conditions should, in theory, make us feel distressed since the *sukka* seems to represent the vulnerability of Man. So why command us to be joyful, precisely at a time when one is confronted with all that can go wrong in life?

Here another question comes to mind. Since the *sukka* teaches us about life's handicaps, we would expect that Jewish law would also require its interior to reflect a similar message. As such, the *sukka* should be empty of all comfort. It should just contain some broken chairs, an old table and some meager cutlery to eat one's dry bread with.

However, Jewish law holds a great surprise. It stipulates that the *sukka*'s interior should reflect a most optimistic lifestyle. Its frail walls should be decorated with beautiful art, paintings and other decorations. The leaking roof, made from leaves or reeds, should be made to look attractive by hanging colorful fruits from it. One is required to bring one's best furniture into the *sukka*, if possible to place a carpet on the ground, and have nice curtains hanging from its windows. One should eat from the most beautiful plates and use one's best cutlery. Meals should be more elaborate than usual, and should include delicacies. Singing should accompany those meals. All this seems to reflect a feeling that this world is a most pleasant place made for our enjoyment and recreation!

So why sit in a weatherbeaten hut?

The message could not be clearer: however much the *outside* walls and the leaking roof reveal Man's vulnerability and uncertainty, *inside* these walls, one needs to make one's life as attractive as possible and enjoy its great benefits and blessings.

This should not be lost on us. Instead of becoming depressed and losing faith in mankind after the great tragedy in New York, and the ongoing terrorist attacks in Israel, we should continue to approach life with the optimistic note which is conveyed to us by the beautiful interior of the *sukka*. True, the ongoing guerrilla attacks on Jews in the land of Israel, and the awful attack on, and collapse of, the Twin Towers in the heart of a country—which believed it could offer its citizens a great amount of security—proves how vulnerable modern Man really is and how shaken the outer walls of his "*sukka*" are! But this should not hold us back from enjoying life as much as possible. To be happy when all is well is of no great significance. But to be fully aware of the dangers which surround us, while simultaneously continuing our lives with "song and harp," is what makes humans great and proud.

We would therefore do well to discourage people from speculating about "the end of days," or reading kabbalistic and other sources informing us that the messianic days are very close and that the wars preceding the coming of the *Mashiach* are imminent. There is no way of knowing. Just as in the days of Shabbatai Zvi,* such speculations, however tempting, could cause a great backlash and inflict great damage. Instead, we should stay with our feet firmly planted on the ground and make sure we live up to our moral and religious obligations.

The attack on, and collapse of, the Twin Towers should encourage people to unite and to display more sensitivity to each other's needs. It should encourage Jew and gentile to build strong family ties and create, just as in the case of the *sukka*, strong and pleasant homes. It should inspire people to go to synagogue and church, and create cohesive communities, because these are some of the "decorations" in our lifelong *sukka*.

Indeed, the walls of our worldly *sukka* may be shaking, but let us not forget that we have an obligation to decorate its interior.

---

* Shabbatai Zvi was a self-declared Messiah who was responsible for bringing about a great upheaval in the European Jewish community in the seventeenth century. After it became clear that he was a fraud, many Jews became disillusioned with the Jewish traditional sources, which they had regarded as proof that Shabbatai Zvi was indeed the Messiah. Consequently they left the fold.

36

Chanuka: The Religious Equilibrium
of the *Menora*

THE *menora* of *Chanuka*, sometimes called the *chanukiya*, has, as we know, its roots in the *menora* of the Temple. While there are many *halachot* regarding how the biblical *menora* should look, and how it should be built, Rashi points to a most remarkable halachic feature that requires our attention. Regarding the instruction that the lamps need to be arranged in such a way that they are lit "towards the *menora*" (*Bamidbar* 8:2), Rashi comments that this means that all the lamps should point in the direction of the middle light.

The Italian sage and physician, Rabbi Ovadia Sforno, in his masterful commentary on the Torah, argues that this is to teach us that the "right-wingers" and "left-wingers" need to focus on the middle light which is the main light of the *menora*. While both are completely dedicated to Torah and its tradition, the right-wingers, i.e., those who are busy with eternal life, learning and implementing Torah, need to know that without the left-wingers, those who occupy themselves with the affairs of the mundane world, Judaism will not succeed. At the same time, the left-wingers have to understand that without those who occupy themselves with the study and implementation of Torah, their worldly occupation would lack the opportunity of sanctification. Only in a combined effort, symbolized by the middle light, will there be the kind of equilibrium which the Torah and Judaism requires. This is based on the talmudic principle that "If not for the leaves, the grapes could not exist" (*Chullin* 92a).

Rabbi Samson Raphael Hirsch, known for his philosophy of "*Torah im Derech Eretz*," comments on Yaakov's final blessings to his children:

> The nation that is to descend from him [Yaakov] is to be, in its external relations, a single unit and internally a "*Kehal Goyim*," a United Congregation of many kinds of people and professions. Each tribe is to represent a special type of person. The people of Yaakov, who, as Israel, are to reveal to the world the directive power of God, penetrating and conquering everything that is earthly in human beings, is, therefore, not to show themselves as being in any way one-sided, but, as a model nation, shall present in a nutshell the most varied appearance of all different characteristics. In its tribes, martial nations as well as merchant ones, agricultural nations as well as scientific and scholarly ones etc., are all to be represented. Thus the fact is to be made clear to the world that the devotion and sanctification of human life in the bond with God through His law is not dependent on, or conditional to, any special calling in life or national characteristic, but that the whole of mankind, with all its diversity, is called on to accept the one common conception of God, as taught by Israel, and so from all the different individual and national characteristics of mankind into one United Kingdom of God.
>
> (*Bereishit* 35:11–12, Isaac Levy, trans. Judaica Press, 1971)

Chatam Sofer, however, gives this halachic requirement a slightly different meaning. He warns his readers not to deviate from the middle road. As long as Jewish law is fully observed, one should not be too much of a right or left-winger. The ways of God are those which testify to religious balance. This does not mean, as some people would interpret it, that a mediocre attitude towards observance is advocated, or that a kind of religious status quo is maintained in which people no longer strive for higher spiritual dimensions, but that one should understand that it is not becoming religiously "corpulent" that is the ultimate goal, but rather becoming spiritually elevated. To grow "plump" is to become overly right- or left-wing with the result that one topples over; to become elevated means that one grows in equal and straight proportions.

A religious person's greatest failing is to forget what he represents.

– 37 –

Pesach: Judaism's Main Purpose
is to Complicate Life

In *Devarim* (16:1), we find a verse which demands our special attention because of its far-reaching implications for Jewish life, and the meaning of religion, in general:

> *Take care* of the month of the early ripening [*Nissan*] and bring the Pesach offering unto the Lord your God, for in the month of the early ripening, the Lord your God took you out of Egypt at night-time.

As is well known, this verse instructs the people of Israel to make sure that *Pesach*, the holiday which celebrates one of the most important events in Jewish history, the Exodus from Egypt, will always fall in the spring, in the month of *Nissan* (April–May).

Ovadia Sforno adds the following unusual statement:

> [The meaning of this verse is as follows:] Take care, with ongoing attention, that the month of *Nissan* will always fall in the spring by means of the "*ibbur*" (an astronomical calculation which combines the "lunar months" with the "sun years"), so that you adjust the lunar year with the one of the sun.

A careful reading of Sforno's comment reveals a most daring thesis. Since the lunar year consists of less days than the solar year, and since the Jewish year is, to a great extent, based on the lunar year, there is a need, after a few "lunar years," to add, immediately prior to *Nissan*, an extra month (*Adar Sheni*) to make sure that *Nissan*, and therefore *Pesach*, will fall in the spring.

Sforno alludes here to a most important question: Why does the Jewish calendar not simply follow the solar year? If, at any rate, we must make sure that *Pesach* falls in the spring (and *Sukkot* in the autumn), what is the purpose of consistently following a lunar year, if eventually one has to bring these dates into accord with the solar year?

His answer is most telling: in order to ensure that the Jewish people *constantly* supervise and take care of the month of ripening, *Nissan* and the festival of *Pesach*, the Torah *complicated* the Jewish year by modeling it on a lunar year, so that *Nissan* would not *automatically* fall in the spring, thereby forcing the sages and astronomers to devise complicated calculations to make sure that it *does*.

In other words: in reality, there is no reason why the Jewish year had to be founded on a lunar year, but since *Pesach*, the great reminder that God governs every moment of Man's life, should be on the mind of the Jew throughout the whole of the year, God decided to complicate matters by seeing to it that we take notice, with "ongoing care," of God's Providence in the world every day of the lunar year!

We may suggest that Sforno knowingly, or unknowingly, reveals one of the most novel and astonishing concepts of the Jewish Tradition: *Judaism's main purpose is to complicate life*. This is in no way an eccentric observation but is consistent with the very purpose of religious life. *Religion is a protest against taking life for granted* and it is through its demands and constant far-reaching interference into our daily life that it makes Man aware that God is our daily Companion. No doubt God could have made life easy and straightforward, but this would have undermined the very purpose of creation: the searching out and discovery of God at every moment, and on every level, of Man's existence in this world.

This is clearly the meaning behind the statement by Rabbi Chanania ben Akashia when he said: "The Holy One Blessed be He desired to confer merit upon Israel, therefore He gave them Torah and *mitzvot* in abundance, as it is said: 'God desires for the sake of its righteousness that the Torah be expanded and strengthened.' (*Yeshayahu* 42:21) (*Makkot* 23b)."

– 38 –

Pesach: To Roast or to Boil–
That is the Question

THE TORAH does not often give instructions related to food. Besides the laws of *Kashrut*, and those that relate to *Pesach*, there are no instructions on how to prepare food or how to eat it. The only remarkable exception to this is the law concerning the *Korban Pesach*, the Passover lamb.

The Torah commands the members of every Jewish home to roast a lamb and eat it on the eve of the first day of *Pesach* in the Temple in a similar way to how it was eaten at the time of the Exodus of Egypt (*Shemot* 12:1–28; 43–49; *Devarim* 16:1–8).

While on all other occasions, the Torah leaves it up to the human being to decide whether he will eat his food cooked or roasted, the text is, in this instance, most explicit in its instructions that Jews should only eat this meat once it is properly roasted.

> Then you shall eat the meat on that night, roasted with fire; with unleavened bread (*matzot*) and bitter herbs are they to eat it. You may not eat of it half-cooked and also not boiled in water, only roasted with fire, its head with its legs and with its innards.
>
> (*Shemot* 12:8)

What is the difference between cooking and roasting? And why does the Torah emphasize the absolute prohibition to cook or boil the Passover lamb in such uncompromising terms?

Maharal, in his commentary on the *Haggada*, explains that there is a basic difference between cooking (boiling) and roasting. To paraphrase him, cooking is an act which "assimilates" while roasting "separates." When cooking, we draw several other ingredients into the object we are boiling. These ingredients assimilate with the object, and the object itself absorbs, and even adapts itself to the added components. It also expands, absorbing the other ingredients, and becomes soft and begins to disintegrate. Roasting, however, does the reverse: its main function is to expel. Not only does it remove all the blood present, but it also separates all ingredients that are not essential to the meat. As such, it shrinks the meat and makes it tough and impenetrable.

This, explains Maharal, is the symbol behind the *Korban Pesach*. At the time of the Exodus, when the people of Israel are, for the first time, to become a nation, it is not yet possible to allow any absorption from outside. No outer influences that could compromise its essential nature may be permitted. The formation of the nation must involve a courageous stand against the world in which it endured a 210-year exile and reject its culture. As such, it cannot allow any expansion that will weaken its inner structure. It must be solid and impenetrable. This is the time to strengthen its own identity and reject all foreign elements.

We may wonder why the Torah makes this requirement only once a year. Why not place a solid prohibition against all cooking and boiling, since such acts symbolize matters that are in opposition to the essential nature of the people of Israel? Should this not be the logical conclusion of the above? Nevertheless, not only do we not find such a prohibition, but we are actually told about a positive commandment to cook the offering of the *Nazir*, the person who for a limited amount of time denies himself some physical benefits so as to better his spiritual situation. He is commanded to bring an offering including a cooked forefoot of the ram (*Bamidbar* 6:19).

The answer is symptomatic of the Jewish Tradition. Once its foundations have been well established, and the structure of Judaism stands like an unshakable mountain, it is able to weather any unwelcome influence from without, and is capable of absorbing all forms of genuine human wisdom when this will add to a deeper understanding of Judaism and grant the Jew a greater commitment towards the Jewish Tradition. Judaism has never been afraid to confront human wisdom and respond to attacks on its tradition. If it would, it would admit to its own weakness. Attacks by Spinoza, Hegel or

Nietzsche have not shaken its foundations and its fundamental beliefs. Its spokesmen responded with dignity and erudition.

Careful study of the famous work, *Chovot HaLevavot* (Duties of the Heart) by Rabbi Bahya ben Joseph Ibn Paquda, written in the 11th century, proves beyond doubt that the author made use of Islamic mystical concepts.

When Rabbi Mendl of Satenav wrote his famous book on character improvement called *Cheshbon HaNefesh* (Taking Stock of the Soul), it was praised by the greatest rabbinical luminaries of the time. It is, however, certain that the book was based on the works of Benjamin Franklin, the famous eighteenth-century gentile inventor, statesman and author. In his books, he suggested the daily cultivation of 13 virtues and it is clear that these found their way into *Chesbon HaNefesh* by Rabbi Mendl of Satenav. When Rabbi E. E. Dessler, author of the classic work *Michtav MeEliyahu*, was told that some of his observations appeared to be similar to those of Dale Carnegie in *How to Win Friends and Influence People*, he responded: "They are not similar; they are taken from there!" Throughout Jewish history, great sages have used the wisdom of non-Jewish thinkers and scientists to explain and expand on Jewish concepts. Clearly, they were not afraid to do so and were convinced that God had sent knowledge via these non-Jewish scholars to help mankind advance itself and to aid the Jewish Tradition. (See also the works of Rabbi Kook, especially his *Orot HaKodesh*, where he approves of this approach.)

This, however, was only possible after Judaism became well established. When Jews celebrate and reenact the beginnings of Judaism at *Pesach* time, they are reminded that one first needs to solidify its foundation. Once that is accomplished, one is allowed throughout the rest of the year to absorb ingredients from outside. One can see this clearly in the case of the *Nazir*.

Only after he has completed his period of solidification of his commitment toward Judaism is he allowed to offer food that is cooked. First, he needs to put his Judaism once more on a strong base and "roast" his spiritual diet. After that, he will have the strength and the capacity to assimilate his personality with other ingredients.

In these difficult days in the history of the State of Israel, Israelis will have to learn this lesson. To believe that secular culture will provide the answers to Israel's problems is a fatal mistake. Now that Israel is in need of great strength and solidarity, it must, first of all, put its Jewish ideological foundations in order. Only later in time will it be secure enough to allow foreign elements to integrate into its strong tradition. This is not a time for Israel to import foreign elements; if anything, it needs to export its own spiritual values to the gentile world. Were it to do so, it would command great respect in the eyes of the nations of the world—and would rediscover its own self-respect.

39

Shavuot: Torah and Combustibility

ONE OF THE MOST challenging aspects of religious life is how to relate to the concept of revelation. Judaism's uncompromising claim that the Torah is not a book which was authored by man, but rather is the result of a revelation of God's Will towards mankind, requires a formidable amount of faith in the face of much intellectual skepticism and secularity.

Over the last few hundred years, major arguments have erupted concerning the divinity of the text of the Torah. Since the days of Spinoza's *Tractatus Theologico Politicus* (17th century), we have witnessed many Bible scholars who have dissected the Torah in every way possible, concluding that the Jewish claim of its divinity is unfounded and farfetched.

Religious scholars have, of course, tried to refute these theories with heavy artillery. Profound papers have been written in which it has been proven that Spinoza's arguments, and those of others, were erroneous, and often lacked intellectual objectivity.* In our days, a sincere, but problematic, attempt has been made by some mathematicians and Jewish outreach programs to prove the Torah's divinity with the discovery of the "Bible codes" which are presumably found within the biblical text.

Still, the question which needs to be raised is whether this is the right approach. If, as Judaism maintains, the Torah is indeed the ultimate Divine truth, is it at all possible, or even advisable, to take a somewhat "academic"

---

* For a comprehensive treatment of the academic approach towards the Torah, see my books: *Between Silence and Speech*, ch. 10 and *The Written and Oral Torah*, pp. 201–33. Both books were published by Jason Aronson.

approach to verify its divinity? Would not the fact that it is Divine make it totally unreceptive to academic scrutiny and proof? Can this not be compared to trying to study organic matter with the accepted criteria used by scientists when studying inorganic phenomena? Simultaneously, should religious scholars and outreach programs not ask themselves if they are not violating the prohibition to "try the Lord" when they look for definite proofs? (see *Shemot* 17:7).

So how should we substantiate the claim that this text is of Divine origin? If, indeed, it is beyond the capacity of proof, or perhaps it is even prohibited to search for such a proof, what then are the ways to grasp its divinity? Why are we not as convinced as our forefathers were? Is it because we are more "intellectually sophisticated" than they were, and that we possess some inner knowledge they did not have? Many of us may have opted for this opinion, in our conception of the divinity of the Torah, but we should ask ourselves if we are not guilty of self-deception.

Rabbi Yaakov Tzevi Mecklenburg, in his monumental work *HaKetav VeHaKabbalah*, seems to touch on this problem. Commenting on the *quality* of the revelation at Sinai, and quoting the verse: "And the appearance of the glory of God was like a consuming fire (*Aish Ochelet*) on the summit of the mountain before the eyes of the Children of Israel" (*Shemot* 24:17), the venerable rabbi asks what is meant by the expression "a consuming fire?" Does this not indicate a destructive force? Why not simply say that God is like fire?

Reminding us of the fact that at Sinai, Israel had risen to the level of prophecy after it had emerged from a life of misery and spiritual slavery, he continues:

> The truth is that the people of Israel were not all equal in their spiritual level. And they did not see or perceive the same kind of revelation at Sinai. Rather, each one was only able to receive this revelational experience in accordance with the spiritual condition of his soul. Every Jew saw something, but what he experienced was directly proportional to the *preparation* he had put into it. *When a person was less prepared, he only experienced a minimal level of revelation at Sinai. And the one who prepared more received more.* And this is the meaning of a "consuming fire." The perception of God's greatness is exactly the same as the way fire takes holds of various objects. There are items that are by nature combustible and when you touch them with a flame they produce an enormous fire. But, there are other items which when you put a

flame to them remain immune and nothing will happen to them. Just like nature has made certain materials receptive to fire, so it is with the Sinai revelation.

A flame increases or dims depending on the combustibility of the fuel. So it is with the Jew and with all people. *The receptivity of the Jew towards the divinity of Torah is proportional to the preparation he invests into it.* We would suggest that the reason why we are confronted with so much skepticism concerning the Torah's divinity in our days is not at all dependent on intellectual sophistication but on the (subconscious) refusal to be aware of our own level of receptivity. Only through spiritual labor and honesty is one capable of preparing one's self towards this receptivity. This may seem like a comfortable escape when dealing with the issue at hand, but, in truth, it touches on the very essence of Man's spiritual condition. Like music and art, the Torah cannot be approached from the perspective of academic learning. It is the soul's language that is at stake. Fire is unable to penetrate where no potential flame burns. Or as the English expression goes: "Like only finds like."

> "The slenderest knowledge that may be obtained of the highest things is more desirable than the most certain knowledge of lesser things," Aristotle once said.* It would be wise for all parties concerned to stop trying to disprove or affirm the Torah's divinity and, first of all, ask ourselves: Are we or are we not made of material which is combustible to the inner world of the Torah? Once we have transformed ourselves and our souls into spiritual fire, all questions concerning the Torah's divinity will be settled.**

---

* Quoted by Thomas Aquinas, *Summa Theologica* (1:1:5 ad 1).
** For another approach, see: "*Shavuot:* Revelation and Learning."

40

Shavuot: Revelation and Learning

IN *Pirkei Avot* (3:10), we find a rather unbelievable statement by one of the sages:

> Rabbi Dostai ben Yanai said in the name of Rabbi Meir: "Whoever forgets even one thing of his Torah learning, Scripture regards him as though he is liable to pay with his life, for it is said: 'Be careful and guard your life greatly, lest you forget the things you saw [at the time of the revelation at Sinai] with your own eyes, and lest they be removed from your heart your entire lifetime, and you shall inform your children and grandchildren of them, the day you stood before God, your God at Chorev....'"
>
> (*Devarim* 4:9–10)

Why should the failure to remember a part of Torah which one learned give evidence to the fact that one forgot that which one had seen with his own eyes when standing at Sinai? Besides the fact that forgetfulness is a normal human condition, there is also a great difference between the power of sight and the act of learning. In the case of the generation which *actually* stood at Sinai, we understand why such people should be liable. They actually *saw* the revelation at Sinai. But why should those who did not stand at Sinai, and "only" learned Torah which they afterwards forgot, be liable as well? How could Rabbi Dostai compare anybody who lives thousands of years after the revelation with those who actually stood at Sinai?

In his commentary on the Torah, Ramban states that the verse quoted above clearly focuses on the *circumstances* under which the Torah was given and not on the actual contents of the Torah. In that case, it is even more difficult to see how the observation by Rabbi Dostai is borne out by the verse he quotes as his proof. He points out that those who learn the *contents* of the Torah and then forget what they learned are liable to pay with their lives, but his proof is derived from a statement which speaks about the need to keep the *circumstances* under which the Torah was given alive and not about its content.

It is rather interesting to note that the Sinai experience never gave rise to a special day in the Jewish calendar. Although it is true that *Shavuot* is traditionally regarded as the day of the giving of the Torah, it is still remarkable that there is no such connection made in the biblical text—it were the sages who made this connection. *Shavuot* mainly appears as a festival celebrating the new harvest (see *Vayikra* 23:9–22). Neither does the Torah command the Israelites to observe a special *mitzva* with the purpose of reenacting this unique moment in Jewish history. Compare this to the festivals of *Pesach* or *Sukkot*. The historical events which took place on these festivals are translated into numerous *mitzvot*, such as the consumption of *matza* and dwelling in the *sukka*.

We must therefore draw the conclusion that while such festivals as *Pesach* and *Sukkot* need to be *contemporized* every year, there is no such need when dealing with the event of revelation. *Pesach* and *Sukkot* celebrate events which took place in the past; by reenacting them, through observing such commandments as *matza* and *sukka*, the Jew is able to re-experience the moment afresh.

This is not so when we consider the moment of revelation. *There is no need to commemorate the event*! The reason for this is most telling. One does not commemorate something which takes place in the "here and now"—in the same way that it would be an affront to commemorate a human being when he is still with us today.

By refusing to give the revelation at Sinai any commemoration, the Torah makes the crucial point that the revelation at Sinai is not a past experience which needs to be reactivated in the present (like *Pesach* or *Sukkot*). It is an ongoing adventure! At Sinai, the revelation started but it never came to a close. Its words perpetuate and persist. But how does this revelation continue? It continues through the Torah itself, and its study. Learning Torah *is* revelation! The Torah is not the record of that which once happened at Sinai, but that which takes place now while we study it. Granted, the Torah takes its roots at the moment of Sinai when it started to penetrate into our universe, but that moment continues to unfold evermore.

As such, learning Torah is neither the study of what happened a long time ago nor is it what God *once* commanded man to do. Rather it is the confrontation with the Divine word at this *present* moment.

Torah learning consists of components that are radically different to any other study known to Man. It is not a confrontation with a text but with a *voice.* And it is not merely listening to this voice which is required, but a type of higher level of hearing which is achieved through actively *responding* to that voice. This is accomplished through the careful observance of the commandments. It is the Divine voice which is captured and becomes tangible in the fulfillment of the *mitzvot.* "One hears differently when one hears in doing," Franz Rosenzweig, the famous philosopher and *ba'al teshuva,* once observed (Franz Rosenzweig, *On Jewish Learning,* Schocken, NY, 1955). Expressed differently: there is an experiential difference between a secular act of *reading* or *studying* a text and the religious act of *listening* to Torah.

With this in mind, we are now able to understand Rabbi Dostai's observation: one can only forget that which *was,* but one cannot forget what *is.* Learning Torah is equivalent to standing at Sinai. Learning Torah is seeing its contents transmitted at Sinai in the "here and now." So the learning of its text is a religious occurrence, the experience of that which normally can only be recalled. The moment one forgets Torah, one transgresses, "Lest you forget the things which you saw [and should continue to see]." This could not mean anything else but that when one has reached the point where his Torah knowledge may be forgotten, it must be the result of something which he *saw* and not what he *sees!* But when one learns Torah as a religious experience, and one sees its revelation alive, then the gap of several thousand years, from the time when the revelation started and where it finds itself now, no longer exists. As such, the Torah is given every day afresh, and Rabbi Dostai draws our attention to a major tenet of Jewish belief.

41

The Mystery of the Second Day *Yom Tov*

Oɴᴇ ᴏғ ᴛʜᴇ ᴍᴏsᴛ puzzling laws in *Halacha* is the requirement to observe a second day *Yom Tov* in all Jewish communities outside Israel. This means that festivals such as *Shavuot,* which reminds us of the theophany on Sinai, is celebrated for two consecutive days in the Diaspora, while in Israel, as stated in the biblical text, it is only celebrated on one day (see *Shemot* 34:22 and *Devarim* 16:10).

This is due to the fact that in the olden days the Jewish calendar was not yet fixed to the same extent as it is today. In former days, the *Sanhedrin,* the Supreme High Court in Jerusalem, would declare a new month after eyewitnesses testified that they had just seen the new moon in its first appearance. Immediately, the court would declare this day the first day of the new month.

Since this information would not always travel fast enough to Jewish communities outside the land, it became necessary for these communities to observe two consecutive days of *Yom Tov.* The reason for this is that a Jewish month can only consist of 29 or 30 days. In that case, there could only be a difference of one day on which the festival would fall. And since biblical festivals always have a fixed date (as stated by the Torah), a two-day celebration became necessary.*

This law is still applicable today. Consequently, any Jew living outside

---

* For a short overview of this complicated issue see: *Yom Tov Sheni Kehilchato* by Rabbi Yerachmiel David Fried and *The Book of our Heritage*, by Rabbi Eliyahu Kitov, vol 1., *Rosh Chodesh.*

the land of Israel is required to observe two days of *Yom Tov*, such as on *Pesach*, *Shavuot* and *Sukkot*.

The difficulty with this rabbinical decree today, however, is that since the days of Hillel HaNassi (4th century BCE), an official and fixed calendar (no longer in need of eyewitnesses) has been in operation and, consequently, there is no longer any doubt as to which is the correct day of *Yom Tov*. It is for this reason quite surprising that the sages did not annul the second day *Yom Tov*, but insisted on its continuation.

The classical answer given is that since this had been the official *minhag* for so many years, and had become so well established that an annulment would no longer be possible.

The *Netziv* suggests a completely different approach in his *Ha'emek Davar*, which to many will be an important eye-opener:

In *Parashat Emor* (*Vayikra* 22:31), we are introduced to the festivals of the Jewish year with the following seemingly superfluous words:

> And you shall keep My commandments, and You shall do them, I am the Lord.

Netziv states that this verse is intended in its meaning to instruct the sages to make a fence around these festivals and to strengthen them by decreeing a second day *Yom Tov* to be observed outside the land of Israel.

In his notes, entitled *Harchev Davar*, *Netziv* quotes a statement from the *teshuvot* of Rabbi Hai Gaon, one of the greatest halachic authorities of the tenth century, which states that the requirement to keep a second day *Yom Tov* outside Israel was already alluded to by the prophets. He concludes with the following words: "And perhaps this was done since the days of Yehoshua ben Nun [Joshua] for those who lived outside [of Israel]."

Netziv then comments that in principle there should never have been any reason to keep a second day of *Yom Tov* outside Israel, even during the time when there was no fixed calendar. His argument is that Jewish law always follows the majority in all matters of halachic doubt, and since in most cases the Jewish month consists of 29 and not 30 days, there is no reason to keep a second day *Yom Tov*. *Netziv* continues and proves his point by stating that we would otherwise encounter a serious contradiction. Why do we not keep two days *Yom Kippur*? And we could no doubt ask why, when counting the *Omer* (the 49 days between *Pesach* and *Shavuot*) (see *Shemot* 34:21), do we only count one date and not two? (After all, if *Pesach* would have started one day later, we also should have started counting the *Omer* a day later.) In that case, we should, for example, say (outside the land of Israel): "Today it is the 31st or the 32nd day of the *Omer*." This is, however, not done, and is, in fact, forbidden. So, why does the *Halacha* insist on a second day *Yom Tov* outside the land of Israel?

Netziv therefore responds that the above verse: "And you shall keep My commandments, and you shall do them" comes to teach us that we should be extremely careful in observing these festivals, and should therefore observe two days outside the land of Israel and not rely on the fact that most months have only 29 days. The meaning of the verse should then be interpreted: "And you shall *surely* keep them in the best way possible and not allow for any doubt."

What, however, could be the spiritual reason for observing two days of *Yom Tov* outside Israel? Is it to ensure that we celebrate them properly?

Rabbi Menachem Recanati, one of the great kabbalists of the 13th–14th century, offers a most original insight. He tells us that it is impossible to be as fully inspired by a particular festival *outside* the land of Israel as one is when one lives *inside* the land of Israel. Israel infuses its own unique spirituality into any festival, and in one day, one is able to reach great spiritual heights. Outside Israel, however, where the spiritual environment is not conducive to this kind of soul-state, one needs two days to achieve the same goal.

We may now understand why there is no requirement to observe two days of *Yom Kippur*. This is not only due to the fact that most people will not be able to fast for such a long time, but also because *Yom Kippur*, due to its extraordinary nature, is able to offer us the opportunity to achieve the same spiritual religious experience outside Israel as that of someone living in the land of Israel. On this day, the soul of a Jew should, and could, be on such a level as if it dwells in the Holy Land—and therefore no second day is required.*

In that case, it is erroneous to argue in favor of a one-day *Yom Tov* outside the land of Israel. Modern interpretations of Judaism, with their emphasis on greater spiritual quality, should, instead of condemning this institution,

---

* The reverse is true regarding the counting of the *Omer*. While *Yom Kippur* is able to offer us great spirituality—even to the point that there is no need for a second day outside Israel—the counting of the *Omer* would offer no more spiritually if a second counting was added each time the *mitzva* was done.

only welcome such a rabbinical enactment, since the quality of life in the Diaspora in modern times has (with all its beauty) definitely not been conducive to greater spiritual opportunities.

42

Tisha B'Av: A Foretaste and
the Eye of a Needle

ONE OF THE MOST puzzling dimensions of Jewish Tradition is the institution of the sacrificial rites in the Temple. Although there are, within the Temple, many other purposes, it cannot be denied that sacrifices stand at the very heart of the Temple service. Vast differences of opinion exist between the early and later commentators regarding how to understand the institution of sacrifices.*

Even more perplexing is the Torah's demand that these sacrifices need to be "*re'ach nichoach laShem.*" Normally these words are translated as meaning "a pleasant aroma to the Lord." Commentators are troubled by this strange phrase, especially since it is mentioned repeatedly throughout the biblical chapters related to the sacrifices. What could such an expression mean? Since when does the Lord need to be approached with perfumes so as to make Him favorable to our requests? Such simplistic interpretations, we believe, turn Judaism into a kind of superstitious tradition, not far different from pagan cults.

The question becomes even more pertinent when we realize that this expression is indeed central to the sacrifices and, therefore, to the very essence of the Temple. There is little doubt that the definitive explanation of this

---

* For a discussion of these positions see: Rabbi Meir Simcha HaCohen of Dvinsk in his commentary, *Meshech Chochma,* Introduction to *Vayikra.*

unusual expression was stated by Rabbi Eliezer Ashkenazi (16th century) in his work, *Ma'asei Hashem* (The Works of God):*

> The phrase "a pleasant aroma to the Lord" does not reflect the absolute quality of the sacrifices, but, on the contrary, it conveys a possible flaw in their nature. In case the worshiper imagines that he indeed has achieved atonement for his sin by just offering a sacrifice, the Torah tells him that this is far from true. The sacrifice is only a "pleasant aroma" which means: *a foretaste for what is yet to come.* If the worshiper does not repent, then the Almighty will say, "Of what purpose are your sacrifices to Me?" (*Yeshayahu* 1:11). The concept of aroma is attributed to the Almighty because of its metaphoric connotation. Just as a pleasant aroma coming from afar bears witness to something good in the offing, so every time the Torah uses the phrase "a pleasant aroma" in connection with the sacrifices, [the meaning is that] it should be to the Almighty as a foretaste of the good deeds which the worshiper is planning to perform. It is called a "pleasant aroma" because anything which can be detected by the senses before it actually arrives at a person is called a smell, e.g., to be "in the air," as it says in the book of *Iyov* (39:25): "He smelled the war from afar," which implies that he sensed the battle even before he actually reached it. Every human being who wants to bring a sacrifice should know that this should be done so as to reconcile himself with God. Consequently the sacrifice is to be brought as a foretaste of good deeds which are still to come.

It is in this light that we have to understand the purpose of the Temple. The Temple service is *not* the ultimate form of worship about which Judaism dreams, but only its beginning, a foretaste of what still needs to come. Its purpose is to function, through metaphoric rites, as a medium through which people are stimulated to make their first steps towards an inner transformation. The Temple is to be an educational institution. In that sense, it offers Man the first step in the right direction towards perfection, but not its culmination. This, after all, has to take place within the heart of a person and be evident in their deeds outside the Temple court.

When the Temple's educational purpose is no longer understood, or is rejected, its existence is no longer of any value. For thousands of years, on

---

* See also Rabbi Yaakov Tzevi Mecklenburg, *Haketav VeHaKabbalah, Vayikra* 1:5.

the date of the destruction of the Temple, Jews have adopted the custom of fasting so as to remind themselves that the first step to real spirituality and repentance is to renew their desire to create a foretaste.

It is not the culmination of repentance that needs to be achieved, but its sincere commencement. This is what the sages had in mind when they said, in the name of God, "Open Me a gate of repentance the size of the eye of a needle, and I will open for you large gates through which infinite light will enter" (*Shir Hashirim Rabbah* 5.3).

VI. Israel and the Jewish State

– 43 –

The Holocaust: Divine Retribution?

F OR SOME YEARS NOW, major debate has surfaced among religious thinkers as to whether the Holocaust should be seen as a Divine punishment.
Pointing to the Torah's warnings (*Vayikra* 26, *Devarim* 28) that the Divine
curses would come true if a widespread violation of the laws of the Torah
would occur, some thinkers maintain that the Holocaust is clearly the result
of the Jewish people transgressing the laws of the Torah.

Looking into these verses, and reading their midrashic comments, it
would indeed be difficult to deny the marked similarity between what happened in the Holocaust and the predictions of the Torah.

Nevertheless, this position could be challenged. Rabbi Yeshaya Karelitz,
z"l, one of the greatest halachic authorities of our generation, known for his
multi-volume halachic works entitled *Chazon Ish*, discusses the problem of
heresy and deliberate violation of Jewish law and its halachic consequences in
today's society. In days of old, heretical views or deliberate violations of Torah
law were penalized, and people guilty of such views or deeds were excluded
from joining some of the community's religious ceremonies or from fulfilling
certain religious functions. Now, however, such halachic rulings, according to
Rabbi Karelitz, *z"l*, could no longer be applied without hesitation:

> [Such laws] only applied at times when the Divine presence was clearly
> revealed, such as in the days when there were open miracles, and a heavenly
> voice was heard and when the righteous would operate under direct Divine
> intervention which could be observed by anybody. Then the heretics were
> of a special deviousness, bending their evil inclination towards immoral

desires and licentiousness. In such days there was [the need] to remove this kind of wickedness from the world, since everybody knew that it would bring Divine retribution onto the world [including] drought, pestilence and famine. But at the time of "Divine hiding," in which faith has become weak in people, there is no purpose in taking such action [harsh measurements against heretics and violators]; in fact it has the reverse effect and will only increase their lawlessness and be viewed as the coercion and violence [of religious fanatics]. And therefore we have an obligation to try to bring them back with "cords of love." (*Hoshea* 11:4)

(*Chazon Ish, Yoreh Deah, Hilchot Shechita* 2:16)

This unprecedented statement is, we believe, of major importance. *Chazon Ish* maintains that we cannot compare our own times, in our exilic state, to the earlier days, specifically the biblical periods. In these earlier days, faith was strong and people did not doubt its foundations. Divine intervention was clear and consequently there was no reason why one should doubt God's existence and the truth of His Will as stated in the Torah. Heresy and the violation of the Torah's precepts could, therefore, only be the result of deliberate rebellion against better knowledge. One *knew* that one was violating the words of the living God, since no doubt existed concerning His existence and Will. As such, there were proper reasons to take action against those who broke the covenant and spoke heresy. They knew that they were falsifying the truth. It was purely their physical desires which made them travel down this road.

This, however, is no longer the case. God's presence is no longer as conspicuous as it was, and much of what happens to mankind appears to be random, without any indication that it is the work of the Lord of the Universe. Therefore, one can no longer call heretical views the result of deliberate viciousness. These views may, in fact, be the honest consequence of careful deliberation which is clouded by the confusion of not knowing how to see and understand the workings of history and matters such as personal tragedy.

For several centuries, so-called "academic studies" of the Torah have undermined its authenticity, convincing many well-intentioned individuals to believe that there was proof that the Torah did not reflect the Will of God. As such, there was no longer a reason to live by its precepts.

This is no longer deliberate heresy but intellectual confusion.

As such, it is difficult to argue that the Holocaust was caused by Divine anger against the violations of Torah precepts and deliberate heresy. The curses in the Torah are meant to come down on those who, against better knowledge and with the full understanding that they were violating the will of God, decided to do so—not on those who are confused or are the victims of others' misunderstandings. This, we believe, is the implication of the words of Rabbi Yeshaya Karelitz *z"l*, in relation to the question of whether the Holocaust should be seen as Divine retribution.

44

The Danger of Holiness
and the Future of Israel

N O WORD IN THE TORAH is as central to Judaism as the word, "*kedusha*," holiness. But no word in the Jewish Tradition is as open to potential misunderstanding.

When discussing sexuality, food consumption and general human behavior, the Torah calls on the people of Israel never to forget that everything needs to be sanctified and consecrated. The ultimate goal is to turn the whole nation into a holy people: "You shall be holy, because I, the Lord your God, am holy" (*Vayikra* 19:2).

This call is repeated many times: "Hallow yourselves, therefore, and be holy, for I am the Lord your God" (ibid., 20:7–8); "And you will be holy unto Me" (ibid., 20:26).

For hundreds of years, serious debate has surfaced among Jewish philosophers concerning whether the Jewish people is *inherently* or only *conditionally* holy. Whatever the answer to this problem may be, the above verses make one point abundantly clear: there is no opportunity or justification for any Jew to hide behind holiness which is not the product of an intensive effort to live an exalted moral life. Any view which exempts the Jew of his responsibility to observe the laws of the Torah—because he is automatically considered to be holy—is heretical and subsequently condemned. The Jew has no claim to anything that he has not earned through hard spiritual work and commitment. This is true as far as the possession of the land of Israel or any other matter is concerned. There are no automatic rights or claims based on holiness—even when one would argue that holiness is inherent—if the people of Israel do not show themselves to be holy in deed and thought.

The sages were well aware of the danger of using the concept of inherent holiness as a way of justifying what in fact is unjustifiable. We see this in their choice of the *Haftarot* which are read on the Shabbat of *parashiot Acharei Mot* (*Vayikra* 16–18) and *Kedoshim* (19–20)—those portions of the Torah which deal with the call for holiness.

There are altogether three *Haftarot* for these two *parshiot*. The one which is read on a given Shabbat depends on whether the *parshiot* are read together or separately, and on whether the congregation follows the Sephardi or Ashkenazi custom.

The *Haftara* which is read when the *parshiot* are combined discusses the equality of all humans and Israel's mistaken view of its exclusive status because of its history and inherent holiness: "Are you not as the Ethiopians to Me, O Israelites? True, I brought Israel up out of the land of Egypt, but also the Philistines from Caphtor and the Arameans from Kir...." (*Amos* 9:7). In other words, the fact that God brought the Jews up from Egypt is not *so* unique a phenomenon that it sets Jews *totally* apart from the rest of the nations. The *Haftara* continues with a harsh statement which removes any possible conclusion that Israel can safely rely on its holiness when it sins: "For I will give the order and shake the house of Israel through all the nations as one shakes sand in a sieve and not a pebble falls to the ground. All the sinners of My people shall perish by the sword, those who say: 'Never shall evil overtake us to come near to us.'"

Amos continues: "The eyes of the Lord God are upon the sinful kingdom, and I will wipe it off the face of the earth, yet I will not utterly destroy the house of Yaakov, says the Lord" (9:8). While we see within this verse a promise that a remnant of Israel will survive, there is no promise that the Jewish people will in any way be protected beyond their basic survival, or will be able to make a claim on the land, or anything else, when it does not observe the laws of the Torah.

The other two *Haftarot* carry a very similar message: when the people of Israel behave in evil ways, "when Jerusalem sheds blood in its midst," when the people will "disdain father and mother" and "oppress the stranger," "violate the woman in her period," "take usury and interest," then "I will scatter you among the nations and disperse you throughout the lands, I will consume the uncleanness out of you. You shall be dishonored in the sight of the nations and you shall know that I am the Lord" (*Yechezkel* 22:15–16).

These *Haftarot* are clearly a protest against all those who claim that the nation of Israel is inherently holy and is consequently able to lower its standards of behavior or permit itself deviation from morality. What indeed characterizes the people of Israel as separate and unique is nothing other than the result of its undivided commitment to live a life of holy deeds.

When contemplating the reestablishment of the State of Israel after nearly 2,000 years of exile, no Jew should believe that the land is guaranteed to remain his forever. It could easily be taken away as it has been in the past. And no army, law or international body will be of any help.

45

The Palestinians' Claim to the Land of Israel
A Serious Warning

Tractate *Sanhedrin* (91a) contains a most relevant story which took place in the fourth century BCE during the days of Alexander of Macedonia, known as Alexander the Great. Just after Moshe's death, when Yehoshua entered the land of Israel together with his people, there were seven tribes, hostile to the Jews, that were occupying the land. Yehoshua offered them the prospect of staying in the country and living in peace with the Israelites with full security on the condition that they would commit themselves to the seven commandments of Noach, the moral code for all humanity.* If, however, they chose not to do so, they would have the option of leaving. Thereupon he led his people into the land, and war broke out, since most tribes refused to opt for either suggestion. Only the Canaanites left earlier and seem to have settled in Africa (*Rambam, Melachim* 6:5).**

Hundreds of years later, the Canaanites came to Alexander's international court with a claim that the land of Israel should be returned to them. When the court inquired into their reasons, the Canaanites, also called the "*Bnei* Africa" (the inhabitants of Africa), said that they were forced out of the land by the Israelites in the days of Yehoshua and that this injustice should

---

* For a full discussion of these laws see my book: *The Written and Oral Torah: A Comprehensive Introduction* (NY: Jason Aronson, 1998) pp. 39–45.
** Others say it was the Girgashites who fled to Africa while the Canaanites fled to Germany! (*Radak* on *Ovadia* 1:20.)

be rectified. When Alexander asked them for proof of their claim to the land, they responded that it was the Torah of the Jews which in fact supported it. Did it not say, "The land of Canaan with the coasts thereof"? (*Bamidbar* 34:2). And since Canaan was their forefather, they had a legitimate claim to return to the land and take possession of it.

Consequently, Alexander (who is known to have been somewhat sympathetic to the Jews) turned to the sages with a request to respond. One Jewish ignoramus by the name of Gebiha ben Pesisa, known for his great love for his fellow Jews, asked that *he* defend the Jewish claim to the land against the Canaanites. "Authorize me to go and plead against them before Alexander of Macedonia. Should they defeat me, then [you can] say: 'You have defeated an ignoramus from among us,' and if I defeat them, then say: 'The Torah of Moshe has defeated them.'" After the sages decided to give him their approval, Gebiha ben Pesisa said to the Canaanites, "From where do you derive your proof?" "From the Torah!" they responded. "In that case, I will also bring a proof from the Torah, for it says that at the time that Cham, one of Noach's children, had uncovered his father's nakedness, Noach said: 'Cursed be Canaan, a servant of servants shall he be unto his brothers' (*Bereishit* 9:25)." (Canaan is another name for the children of Cham.) Gebiha ben Pesisa then explained that due to this curse, the Canaanites had become slaves to the Jews since they are the children of Shem, one of the other sons of Noach to whom the curse refers. In that case, the land would at any rate belong to the Jews, since "Whatever a slave acquires belongs to the master." "Moreover," he said, "you have not served us for years!" Then Alexander said to them [the Canaanites], "Answer him." "Give us three days," they responded; they looked but found no answer. And they left.

When carefully studying this incident, several matters require our attention. First of all, it is rather obvious that the Canaanites were guilty of reading the Torah selectively. Had they "turned the page" they would no doubt have found that the land had already been promised to Avraham in earlier days and that the Torah continually makes the point that God willed it to the Jews. Even more mysterious is the defense of Gebiha ben Pesisa. Why did he use the curse on Cham as his proof? Why did he not use the most obvious argument that was mentioned before—that the Torah makes it abundantly clear that the land was given to the Jews? He could have quoted a multitude verses to back up his claim!

Maharasha, in his commentary, argues that the motivation behind the

Canaanites' claim was much more sophisticated than one might imagine. The Canaanites had read the Torah most carefully and were well aware of the promise that God had made to the Israelites concerning the land. They, however, reminded Alexander's court that they, the Canaanites, had been forced out of the country because of their immoral behavior. The Holy Land had no longer been able to contain them and had consequently spit them out. But, continued the Canaanites, the Israelites had become just as evil as they had been!! The Jewish nation had also become disobedient and had violated the moral code. Even more so, had not the Torah made it abundantly clear that the Jews would only merit the land when they would be a holy nation as demanded by the Torah? In that case, the Jews no longer had a claim to the land and they, the Canaanites, having lived there prior to the Jews, were fully entitled to claim it back!

Even an ignoramus such as Gebiha ben Pesisa understood the Canaanites' argument and had to concede the validity of their claim. So there was no point in quoting verses which stated that God had promised and bequeathed this land to the Israelites in much earlier days.

While the Divine promise, as such, would never completely disappear, its heavenly implementation, together with its Divine protection, could no longer be relied upon. Only after Jews would once more commit themselves to the values of the Torah, would the promise to return to Israel and live in peace be reactivated. It is for this reason that Gebiha ben Pesisa could only make use of the earlier roundabout argument.

When asserting their claim to the land, Jews would do well to realize that the Canaanites' claim still stands and that the above story is not a little telling.

While it may no longer be the Canaanites making this claim, any tribe or nation that ever lived in this country may remind Jews that they can never consider the land of Israel as their unchallenged possession as long as they do not live up to the moral standards of the Torah.

46

Concerning the New Millennium
A Jewish Child and a Wave of the Hand

WHILE JEWS WILL NOT celebrate a millennium for another 240 years, it would be wise to contemplate for just a moment the celebrations which recently took place in the non-Jewish world. The festivities surrounding the birthday of Jesus and his *brit mila* on the first day of January are more than surprising. The astonishing fact that one Jewish child seems to have been at the center of an unprecedented worldwide celebration in which billions of people participated should make us wonder what this is all about.

Rambam informs us that there must be more than a little religious meaning in all this. In his *Mishneh Torah* (*Hilchot Melachim* 11:4), he states that God caused Jesus to have such a great influence on mankind so that people would become accustomed to the concept of the coming of the real *Mashiach*. The great Rav Avraham Yitschak Kook even went so far as to call Jesus a man with "awesome personal power and spiritual flow," which was misdirected and led to his confusion and apostasy. (See: *Sefer Derech HaTechia*, and his letter of June 29, 1913 to the famous scholar, *Ridbaz*, Rabbi Yaakov David Wilovsky.)

Most astonishing is the recounting in the Talmud of the story about how Jesus became an apostate:*

---

* Several scholars state that the identity of Jeshu as Jesus is in dispute. See, for example, Rabbi Yechiel of Paris (*Vikkuach*, R. Margoliot ed., 1920, 16f). See also "Rabbi Yaacov Emden, Bilaam and Jeshu."

Our rabbis teach us: Always let the left hand repel and the right hand invite...unlike Rabbi Yehoshua ben Perayah who repulsed Jeshu [Jesus] with both hands.... When King Janai killed our sages, Rabbi Yeshoshua ben Perayah [and Jeshu] fled to Alexandria in Egypt. When peace resumed, Rabbi Shimon ben Shetach sent a message to him: "From me [in Jerusalem], the city of holiness, to you, Alexandria, my sister: 'My husband stays in your midst, and I sit forsaken.'" He [Rabbi Yehoshua ben Perayah] arose [to return to Jerusalem] and went and found himself in a certain inn, where great honor was given to him. He said: "How beautiful is this *achsania* (inn)." Thereupon Jeshu said to him, "Rabbi, her eyes are narrow." [The word "*achsania*" means "inn" or "innkeeper." Jeshu seems to have thought that Rabbi Yehoshua was speaking about the female innkeeper.] So, Rabbi Yehoshua said to him: "Villain, do you behave yourself like that [looking at women]?" He sent out four hundred trumpets and excommunicated him. He [Jeshu] came before him and said to him: Receive me [let me repent and accept me]. But he would not acknowledge him.

One day he [Rabbi Yehoshua] was reciting the *Shema* and he [Jeshu] came before him. He intended to receive him [to forgive him], and he made a sign to him. He [Jeshu] thought that he repelled him [thinking that the sign was dismissive]. He went and hung up a tile and worshiped it. He [Rabbi Yehoshua] said to him: "Return," but he replied: "So I have understood from you that every one who sins and causes the multitude to sin has no chance to repent."

(*Sanhedrin* 107b)*

There is much in this passage that is unclear. One of the problems is the question of whether this story is suggesting that *if* Rabbi Yehoshua ben Perayah would have been more tolerant towards Jeshu, the latter would not have become an apostate, a false *Mashiach*, and Christianity would never have come about?

Whatever the Talmud may have in mind, one is unable to ignore the fact that it seems to teach us that one erroneous wave of the hand is enough to initiate an unprecedented outburst of animosity which may result in a new or false religion or movement. Ramban notes this in his commentary on the

---

* This passage in the Talmud was once censored by the Church, but is now printed in all the new editions. See *Ma'amar Al Hadpasat haTalmud* by R. R. N. Rabbinowicz, 1952.

event in which Sarai afflicted Hagar, which resulted in an ongoing hatred of Arabs for Jews (see *Bereishit* 16).* The Talmud makes the same observation in relation to the Amalekites, where it discusses the source for Amalek's hatred of Jews as being an unnecessary rejection of his mother by the forefathers (see *Sanhedrin* 99b). In all these cases, a minor mistake resulted in a major, and often outspoken, anti-Semitic ideology.

In his celebrated work, *Makor Baruch*, the well-known sage and Torah commentator Rabbi Baruch haLevi Epstein, author of *Torah Temima*, notes that a harsh and erroneous approach to those who are on the verge of "leaving the fold" has often caused a great deal of damage. In the tractate *Chagiga* (15a), we read the story of Elisha ben Avuyah who, after a certain incident, questioned Jewish Tradition and stopped being religious. The sages are recorded as saying, "'Return, backsliding children (*Yirmiyahu* 3:14) except for Acher [the other one—the name they gave Elisha ben Avuyah after he turned away from Judaism]" implying that he could not repent. As a result of this, Elisha left his people forever.

Most interesting is the following comment made by Rabbi Epstein:

> This phenomenon, to our sadness, seems to repeat itself in every generation. Whenever people quarrel over matters related to ideology and faith, and a person discovers that his more lenient opinion is in the minority, all too often—although his original view differed only slightly from the majority—the total rejection he experiences pushes him over the brink. Gradually, his views become more and more irrational and he becomes disgusted with his opponents, their Torah and their practices, forsaking them completely.
>
> (ch. 13:5)

Rabbi Epstein goes on to discuss the case of Uriel Da Costa (a Dutch Sephardi Jew of the early sixteenth century who denied the authenticity of Oral Law) and alludes to the case of the well-known Dutch apostate and philosopher, Baruch Spinoza, although he does not mention him by name. He criticizes the religious Jewish leaders of the city of Amsterdam who excommunicated both these men:

---

* See also "The Birth of Amalek: The Making of An Enemy."

...instead of instructing him [Uriel da Costa] with love and patience and extricating him from his maze of doubts by showing him his mistake, they disparaged and ridiculed him. They pursued him with sanctions and excommunication, cursing him until he was eventually driven away completely from his people and his faith and ending his life in a most degrading way [Uriel Da Costa committed suicide].*

While Uriel Da Costa did not inflict permanent damage against Judaism, Spinoza became the father of a major philosophical school which *did* cause great damage to the image of Judaism, later encouraging anti-Jewish outbursts, just as in the case of Jesus and his followers (see for example: Emile Fackenheim, *To Mend the World*, Schocken, 1982, ch. 2.).

We indeed wonder what would have happened if religious leaders such as Rabbi Yehoshua ben Parayah and the religious leaders of the Amsterdam Portuguese-Spanish community would have displayed more patience and tolerance. Perhaps Spinoza would not have engendered so much animosity towards Judaism, and Jesus may have stayed in the fold. It would not have led to such virulent Christian anti-Semitism in later days and, with tongue in cheek, we would not have had to deal with the "Year 2000 Bug" which cost us millions of dollars and which drove virtually entire societies to an unprecedented panic. Who would have imagined that one hand, waved nearly two thousand years ago, at a Jewish boy, could ever cause such upheaval in our own days?

---

* For a full treatment of this in relation to Spinoza, see *Spinoza: A Life,* Steven Nadler, (Cambridge, 1999), ch. 6.

– 47 –

Rabbi Yaacov Emden, Bilaam and Jeshu

It is extremely difficult to know, as we indicated in our previous thought, whether the stories and observations about Jeshu in the Talmud actually refer to the Jeshu of the New Testament (NT). Several dates do not correspond, and many other discrepancies manifest themselves.

Scholars have made the important observation that there is also a great discrepancy between the picture which emerges of Jeshu from the actual text of the NT and the one developed by the Church. Even in the NT itself, there are several readings which appear to be inconsistent, possibly because of later interpolations. The observations in the Talmud may therefore quite well refer to the Jeshu as projected by the Church, and not based upon the image of him painted in the NT (notwithstanding the inconsistency related to the dating of these stories).

It is, however, the portrait of Jeshu created by the Church which has prevailed as being the most common, and perhaps the most authoritative, in Western civilization. In its need to create a separation between Christianity and Judaism, the Church went out of its way to rewrite the story of Jeshu in such a way that he became a strong opponent of Judaism, and, above all, *Halacha*.

A critical reading of the text in the NT seems, however, to paint a portrait of Jeshu as a conservative person who was not particularly interested in starting a new religion. Scholars are of the opinion that he was not looking for ways to undermine the *Halacha*, as was his disciple Paul. His statements concerning divorce do not support the view that he opposed it entirely, as was stated by the Church. (See for example Matthew 19:9 in comparison with

Mark 10:1–12.) In fact, he seems to adhere to the view of Beit Shammai that a man is only allowed to divorce his wife when she has committed adultery! (*Mishna, Gittin* 9:10). Nor does the well-known incident where he permitted his disciples to pluck ears of corn on Shabbat prove that he favored Shabbat desecration. The text seems to indicate that it may have been a case of *sakanat nefashot*—saving a life (see Mark 2:23–28).*

It may also be deduced that he was not always consistent in his views, or perhaps he was an "*am ha'aretz*," a man with little grasp of the *Halacha*, lacking in-depth knowledge of the Torah. To account for the instances in which Jeshu is quoted as having spoken against halachic standards, scholars seem to agree that this is due to later "reworking" of the original texts (see David Flusser, ibid., chs. 1 and 4).

This may explain why several rabbis of world renown fostered a far more positive attitude towards Jeshu than the talmudic texts seem to indicate. Besides the observation by Rabbi Avraham Yitschak Kook which we quoted in our last chapter, a most remarkable and surprising statement is found in the preface to *Seder Olam* by the famous eighteenth-century halachic authority, Rabbi Yaacov Emden, the *Yavetz*:

> The founder of Christianity conferred a double blessing upon the world. On the one hand, he strengthened the Torah of Moshe and emphasized that it is eternally binding. On the other hand, he conferred favor upon the gentiles in removing idolatry from them, imposing upon them stricter moral obligations than are contained in the Torah of Moshe(!) There are many Christians of high qualities and excellent morals. Would that all Christians would live in conformity with their precepts! They are not enjoined, like the Israelites, to observe the laws of Moshe, nor do they sin if they associate other beings with God in worshiping a triune God. They will receive a reward from God for having propagated a belief in Him among the nations that never heard His name: for He looks into the heart.

It is worthwhile, however, to mention a controversial midrash which portrays Jeshu in a rather uncomplimentary light. On the verse: "There arose no more a prophet in Israel like Moshe, who knew God face to face" (*Devarim*

---

* For another halachic explanation, see Prof. David Flusser, *Jesus*, (The Magnes Press: 1998) p. 58.

34:10), the sages commented with a most unusual observation: "In Israel none arose, but among the gentiles one *did* arise. And who was that? Bilaam, son of Peor" (*Sifri*). (Bilaam was the one who tried to curse the Jewish people while they wandered in the desert. See *Bamidbar* 22–24.) Since it is untenable that this statement is suggesting that Bilaam ever rose to the same spiritual level as Moshe *Rabbeinu*, several commentators propose that the meaning behind these words is that the gentiles also had someone whose function, in regards to the nations of the world, was similar to that of Moshe in Israel. Just as Moshe was hailed as a great halachic legislator in the eyes of the Jews, in the same way Bilaam was considered a notable authority by the gentiles.

While no allusion to this can be found in the Torah text, the midrash quotes a verse from Bilaam's words in his curse-turned-around-blessing of the Jewish people: "God is not a man that He should lie" (*Bamidbar* 23:19). To this, the *Midrash Tanchuma* (in uncensored printings) adds: "Bilaam foresaw that a man would be born from a woman and would proclaim himself a god. Therefore, Bilaam's voice was given the power to inform the gentiles: 'Do not go astray after this man, God is not a man, and if he [a man] says he is God, he is lying.'" In that sense Bilaam became a "legislator" for the gentiles and warned them of the personality of Jeshu as portrayed by the Church.

Even more interesting is an *Aggada* in *Sanhedrin* 106b where a sectarian asked one of the sages: "Do you know how old Bilaam was when he died?" He replied: "It is not actually stated, but since it is written: 'Bloody and deceitful men shall not live out half their days' (*Tehillim* 55:24), he must have been 33 or 34." He rejoined and said: "You have spoken well. I personally have seen Bilaam's chronicle in which it is stated that Bilaam, the lame, was 33 years old when Pinchas the Lista'a killed him."

Obviously one wonders about Bilaam's chronicle. No such book has been documented, but, as one of the later Jewish writers (Geiger) suggested, it may allude to Jeshu. The latter died when he was 33 years old and was killed by Pontius Pilatus. The name Pinchas Lista'a may well be a corruption of Pontius Pilatus. In that case, Bilaam's chronicle may refer to the NT.

− 48 −
The Birth of Amalek
The Making of an Enemy

JUDAISM'S MAJOR ENEMY in biblical times was the nation of Amalek. This nation *was*, and symbolically *is*, the personification of all evil, racism and anti-Semitism. Amalek was seared into the Jewish consciousness as the first enemy the people of Israel encountered after the crossing of the Red Sea. The Amalekites attacked the Jews several times and brought much disaster and destruction. It was not only the fact that Amalek dared to fight the Israelites, but also the strategy which Amalek used, which revealed its moral bankruptcy. They attacked the Israelites from the back, first focusing on the weak and tired people, then drew Israel into immoral sexual practices and, with tactics similar to later forms of anti-Semitism, operated in secrecy (see *Shemot* 17:8–16).

In later days, it was Haman, a direct descendant of the Amalekites, infamous from the *Purim* story in the Book of *Esther*, who once more showed the evil intentions of this nation. Only through miraculous Divine intervention was Israel saved from the hands of this wicked personality.

Who was Amalek? The Torah tells us that the first Amalek was the son of Esav's son Eliphaz (*Bereishit* 36:4). He was the eponymous ancestor of the Amalekite people. Eliphaz had taken a concubine by the name of Timna, the sister of Lotan who was a son of Seir the Horite, dwelling in the land of Seir where Esav had settled. Timna became pregnant and gave birth to a son who was called Amalek.

The Talmud inquires why Timna married Eliphaz and provides us with an unprecedented statement:

Timna desired to become a proselyte, so she went to Avraham, Yitzchak and Yaakov, but they did not accept her. So she went and became a concubine to Eliphaz, the son of Esav, saying: "I would rather be a servant to this people, [the people of Israel] than a mistress of another nation." *From her Amalek was descended who afflicted Israel.* Why so? Because they should not have repulsed her.

(*Sanhedrin* 99b)

This talmudic statement is most surprising. It is, after all, unclear why the forefathers refused to take her under their wings, and why they did not allow her to convert to Judaism, especially when we are informed that they went out of their way to convert many other people (see Rashi on *Bereishit* 12:5).

Most remarkable is the fact that the sages were not afraid to point their finger in the direction of our patriarchs. Their commitment to truth surpassed their love for the patriarchs. They could have suppressed this story, or they could have stated that Timna was indeed unworthy. The fact that they did not take that road shows their integrity and uncompromising objectivity when truth is at stake.

We do not know of another tradition which has shown such integrity when dealing with its heroes. What is even more surprising is that they considered the refusal by our patriarchs to accept Timna into Judaism as the prime reason for Israel's later affliction the offspring of the first Amalek.

This reminds us of Ramban's statement when he discusses the reasons why the Arab nations show so much hatred for the Jewish people. After Hagar has become pregnant by Avraham, and is now looking down on Sara (who could not become pregnant), Sara complains to Avraham about her:

Then Avraham said to Sara: "See, your handmaid is in your hands, do to her that which is good in your eyes." Then Sara was hard on her and she [Hagar] fled from before her.

(*Bereishit* 16:6)

Ramban's comment is most telling:

Sara our mother sinned in dealing harshly with her handmaid and Avraham, too, by allowing her to do so. God heard her [Hagar's] afflictions and gave her a son who was destined to be a lawless person, who [because of this] would bring suffering on the seed of Avraham and Sara with all kinds of affliction.

In later days, it was Rabbi Shmuel Mohilewer, rabbi of Bialystock and one of the great leaders of the Chibbat Zion movement in the nineteenth century, who made a similar comment when the Turkish government was about to banish from Palestine those Russian Jews who had moved to the country but had not taken Ottoman citizenship. He cried out and said: "It is because of 'Drive out this handmaiden [Hagar] and her son' [21:10] that the Muslims—the children of Yishmael—the son of Hagar, would now cast out the sons of Sara from our land."

Once more we are confronted with an unflinching commitment to truth. Even when running the risk of putting our spiritual heroes into a compromising light, the sages did not shrink from criticizing the patriarchs. And, once more, we are confronted with a daring statement that it is because of the actions of our patriarchs and matriarchs that Jews, thousands of years later, still encounter the hostility of their enemies.

On another occasion, the sages again spoke of the injustice committed against the ancestors of Haman. They stressed that much of Haman's hatred for Jews resulted from the way Yaakov had dealt with his brother Esav, the grandfather of the first Amalekite. In the words of the Book of Esther:

And Mordechai understood all that was done, and Mordechai tore his clothes and put on sackcloth with ashes. He went out into the midst of the city and cried a loud and bitter cry.

(ch. 4:1–2).

The *Midrash Rabbah* courageously makes the following observation:

One bitter cry did Yaakov cause Esav to cry [when the latter was informed by his father Yitzchak that the blessings which were originally meant for him had gone to his brother Yaakov], as it says: "When Esav heard the words of his father, he cried an exceedingly loud and bitter cry" (*Bereishit* 27:34), and it was paid back to him [Yaakov] in Shushan when his offspring [Mordechai] cried a loud and bitter cry [because of the great troubles which Haman, the offspring of Amalek, caused the Jews].

179

This is another instance where the sages point to the fact that it was Yaakov's harsh treatment towards Esav (by "stealing" his blessings of the first-born) which caused the Jews so much pain at the hands of Haman.

Why, indeed, did the sages emphasize this injustice committed by our forefathers? Why not keep quiet? No doubt, they did not want to justify the anti-Semitism of the Amalekites or the Arab nations. Neither did they want to embarrass the patriarchs, knowing quite well that they were men of great spirituality.

We believe that a careful reading of the Torah may provide us with the answer. In *Devarim* (25:19), the Torah demands that Jews "should erase the memory of Amalek from under heaven, thou shall not forget." As is well known, this commandment seems to be a paradox: How can one erase the memory of Amalek if one is not allowed to forget what he did?

However, it is very possible that the Torah hints here not only at the monstrous deeds of Amalek, but also at the injustice of our forefathers when dealing with Esav and Timna. "Erase the memory of Amalek" may well mean that we are obligated to uproot *from within ourselves* the ways in which our ancestors dealt with the ancestors of Amalek. "Do not forget that this behavior was completely unjustified and ultimately caused ongoing pain to your forefathers."

In other words, the Torah teaches us to erase Amalek's memory by making sure that no such nation will ever appear again. *This can only be accomplished when we do not repeat the mistakes of our forefathers.* People create their own enemies and Jews have to teach themselves, and others, to prevent this by all means.

This, however, cannot be done in an instant. It is an ongoing demand which should never be forgotten. This is the meaning of "Erase the memory of Amalek, thou shalt not forget."

The earlier critical observations by our sages are, therefore, most crucial. While there is no way to justify any Amalekite or Arab anti-Semitism in later days, it is most important to understand how such hatred came into existence. By emphasizing the injustice of our forefathers, and the disastrous repercussions which followed, the sages gave us the means to fulfill the *mitzva* of blotting out Amalek's memory by constantly reminding us not to forget how they became our enemies.

VII. The Power of Prayer

Prayer, *Chazanut* and the Cantor*

CONTEMPORARY RELIGIOUS LIFE is fraught with challenges. In a highly secular society, it is no mean feat to stay religious in the authentic sense of the word. This becomes clear, for example, when one enters a synagogue hoping for an uplifting religious experience. Very often, one gets the impression that one has entered the halls of a concert in which a musical performance, consisting of songs of prayer, is taking place, and where decorum is of upmost importance. It is most telling when people, upon leaving the synagogue, remark that it was a "charming service." Such an observation is a tragedy. It reflects a crisis which is occurring in tens of thousands of synagogues throughout the world. In such cases, it is the secular Weltanschauung which has permeated into the world of the synagogue. Since the secular world is unable to cope with matters such as "inner silence," it can do nothing but turn real spirituality into an external performance, and transform a deeply religious service into a showcase. Indifference to the holy is the result.

Most tragic is the role that many cantors play in all this. Instead of realizing that the whole purpose of their *chazanut* is to fight the secularization of the prayers, they have joined the ranks of the secularists. Instead of realizing that God is their audience, they seem to believe that it is the community they need to satisfy.

The task of the cantor, however, is to pierce the armor of spiritual indifference. His purpose is to protest against this apathy through genuine prayer.

---

* The following thought was inspiring by some of the observations from Professor Abraham Joshua Heschel.

His goal is to fight for a communal response, for elevation of souls and for the revelation of the Divine. But what often happens is that the cantor degrades the prayers by transforming his task into a skill, a technical performance. As a result his words only enter into ears, but not into the hearts of the contrite.

Genuine *chazanut* is the art of prayer exegesis. Through the cantor's intonation and heartfelt performance, the community should discover a new meaning in the otherwise all too familiar prayers. Genuine cantorial skill is to resurrect old words and infuse them with new meaning. In a play on words, the Ba'al Shem Tov once remarked that when Noach was told to enter into the *teva* (ark) before the flood started, God told him to also go into the deeper meaning of the "word" (also *teva* in Hebrew). In prayer, a person must enter the word with all that he has and is. It is the task and goal of the cantor to guide the worshiper in this endeavor.

It is here that music enters. The difference between a word spoken and a word sung is that music is the refutation of human finality. Music is an antidote to words becoming slogans. It reaches out to that which lies beyond the capacity of verbal propositions. As such, listening to music is a shattering experience. It propels the listener forward into an aspect of reality, which the mind cannot grasp and a word on its own cannot reach. When listening to *chazanut*, one should become smitten and never recover from the spiritual blow. This is the purpose of *chazanut*. It is an act of resistance against words of prayer becoming stale.

Tradition has it that when a Jew came to the Temple to bring a sacrifice for the atonement of a transgression, the priest would look at him and read his thoughts. If he found that the man had not fully repented, the priest would ask the Levites to chant a melody in order to bring the sinner to full *teshuva*. This should be the task of the cantor.

51

There is No *Mashiach* Without a Song

W HEN ATTENDING SYNAGOGUE SERVICES around the world for prayer, one is often confronted with a lack of religious enthusiasm. In many synagogues, services are heavy and often a little depressing. It is not always the lack of concentration by the worshipers which makes synagogue services unattractive, but the absence of a song and smile. It is true that prayer is a most serious undertaking, yet our sages have often emphasized the fact that the opportunity to speak to the Lord of the Universe is a great privilege which should bring great happiness to Man. After all, for humans, made of flesh and bones, to converse with their Maker is something which has no logical basis. Who is Man to speak to the King of Kings? This is even more true when one contemplates the fact that Man has the opportunity to *praise* God with hymns and laudations. As the great German poet, Johann Wolfgang Goethe, once said, "*Wer einen lobt, stellt sich ihm gleich.*" (He who praises another person places himself on the other's level.) And, as Aristotle, probably referring to Plato, said, "Everyone may criticize him, but who is permitted to praise him?"

Most interesting is the fact that one of the ways we are able to identify the *Mashiach* is in his capacity and willingness to sing. In the tractate *Sanhedrin* (94a), Bar Kapara states that God intended to appoint King Chizkiyahu as the *Mashiach*, i.e., the ultimate redeemer of mankind, but eventually did not.

Chizkiyahu is known as one of the most righteous men the Jewish people has ever seen. He introduced significant religious reforms and was a man of outstanding devotion, committed to the highest level of morality. In fact, he was so successful in his attempt to improve Jewish education that there was "no boy or girl, no man or even woman in the land who was not versed in the religious laws of *tahara* and *tuma*—purity and impurity!"

Still, King Chizkiyahu found himself unable to educate his own son King Menashe in "the fear of God." The latter is known for his wickedness, and commentators observe that this was partially due to the fact that his righteous father did not know how to sing and was, therefore, unable to inspire him. We can be sure that Menashe was well educated in Jewish learning, but all such learning was academic and frigid, because the warmth of a song did not accompany it.

Most telling is the fact that the sages inform us that King Chizkiyahu did not even sing after he experienced a great miracle which saved Israel from the hands of the wicked Sancherib, the Assyrian king.

Not being able to sing is considered by our sages as a serious and irreparable weakness which invalidates one from becoming the *Mashiach*. Indeed we find that all of King Chizkiyahu's efforts to encourage Jewish learning came to an end after he passed away. There is no future to Jewish learning and Judaism without a song and a smile.

This, however, needs some clarification. What is there in a song—that is missing in a spoken word—which makes it so crucial to the Jewish Tradition?

It may be worthwhile to quote a highly irregular statement by the great rationalist thinker, Rambam. Discussing human reason and prophecy, he writes:

> I say that there is a limit to human reason, and as long as the soul resides within the body, it cannot grasp what is above nature, for nothing that is immersed in nature can see above it. Reason is limited to the sphere of nature and is unable to understand what is above its limits…. Know that there is a level of knowledge which is higher than all philosophy, namely prophecy. Prophecy is a different source and category of knowledge. Proof and examination are inapplicable to it. If prophecy is genuine then it cannot depend on the validation of reason…. Our faith is based on the principle that the words of Moshe are prophecy and, therefore, beyond the domain of speculation, validation, argument or proof. Reason is inherently unable to

pass judgment in the area from which prophecy originates. It would be like trying to put all the water in the world into a little cup.

(*Kobetz Teshuvot HaRambam Veiggerotav*, Lichtenberg, Leipzig ed., 1859.
Letter to Rabbi Chisdai, 11, pp. 23a–23b)

Music raises the spoken word to a level which touches on prophecy. It gives it a taste of that which is beyond and transforms it into something untouchable. Just as there is no way to demonstrate the beauty of music to a person who is completely deaf, so is there no way to explain the difference between a spoken word and one which is sung, unless one sings. It lifts a person out of the mundane and gives him a feeling of the imponderable, which is the entrance to joy.

Some men go on a hunger strike in the prison of their minds, starving for God; only song will free them. Prayer is our answer to the inconceivable surprise of living. Abraham Joshua Heschel once said: "To sing is to know how to stand still and dwell upon a word. While this is even true for a song of the individual, it becomes more apparent when a group of human beings join in communal song."

When our sages inform us that no one is able to become the *Mashiach* unless he is able and willing to sing, it should be a message to all who want to be religious that song should be a most important component of their prayers and lives. We are deeply indebted to sephardic tradition, Chassidism and legendary figures such as Rabbi Shlomo Carlebach *z"l*, who have placed song in the center of modern Jewish life. It is time that synagogue rabbis give this aspect of spiritual expression their devoted attention, teaching their community to surprise themselves at what their souls are able to achieve. It is prayer in the form of song which makes that possible.

Camp David and the City of David

July 26, 2000
Tammuz 23 5760

I stand at the *Kotel*, the Wailing Wall.
I see the Wall with Her frozen tears
And Her passing clouds with many sighs.
I read secret books and hundreds of thousands of names.
Names from Egypt, Babylon, Rome, Poland, Spain, Hungary,
America and South Africa.
Names from Auschwitz, Buchenwald and Dachau.
I see the auto-da-fes, the Crusades, the pogroms and the Roman
torture chambers.
Mothers crying about their children,
Women of all ages.
There is also the businessman standing in tears.
The movie star, the politician, the housewife, the yeshiva student
and the strong soldier.

Yeshayahu stands next to me,
A little further on, Rabbi Akiva,
My teachers: Maimonides and Yehuda Halevi, Hillel and Shammai,
Behind me the Gaon of Vilna, occupied with his thoughts
And the Ba'al Shem Tov in deep meditation,
Men, women, children, *Mitnagdim*, *Chassidim*, Ethiopians,

Yemenites, *Sephardim* and *Ashkenazim*,
Jews of all colors.

There is no time, no clock, no early or later.
I stand but cannot grasp.
I say my *tefilla*.
Then the truth descends on me: I know,
I have never left this place.
I find myself here for four thousand years.

The return to Zion is unprecedented,
a happening *sui generis*.
The creation of the State of Israel is a surprise and a shock.
It confuses.
It is a breach in a world where people do not want to be surprised.
And therefore Israel irritates.

The Egyptian, the Babylonian, and the Persian, conquered the world with
much noise, pomp and splendor and disappeared.
The Greek and the Roman, followed with their drumbeat and war car-
riages and died out.
Others came and held their torch high and burned out.
The Jew saw them all, surpassed them all and stayed immortal.

The Jew never left Israel. He was driven out against his will.
Titus and his army.
And the people of Israel protested.
They said "No" to anybody who made a claim.

In his prayers, in his songs, in his home, in the *beit hamidrash*
At the time of his *chupa* and his burial and in his sermons.

Jerusalem.

It is only the Jews who kept on praying for its rebuilding, for 2,000 years
and no other nation.

It is only the Jews who have mourned for 2,000 years for its destruction
and no other nation.

It is only the Jews who fasted and sat on the floor for 2,000 years on the
day the Temple in Jerusalem was destroyed and no other nation.

It is only the Jews who for 2,000 years have broken a glass under their mar-
riage canopy out of sorrow for Jerusalem and no other nation.

It is only the Jews who for 2,000 years have built a house and left one part
of the wall unplastered because of the loss of their Temple
and no other nation.

It is only the Jews whose women do not wear all their jewelry
at once out of reverence for the destruction of Jerusalem and no other
nation.

It is only the Jews who cover their dead with the dust of Israel when they
bring their dear ones to their last resting-place outside the land of Israel
and no other nation.

Is not every Jewish house in exile a piece of Israel on foreign ground?

This is the history, the reality and the future of Israel.

GLOSSARY

Aggada:	Non-legal early Rabbinic literature
Akeida:	Sacrifice of Isaac
Ashkenazim:	Jews who dwelled in North European countries
Avinu Malkeinu:	Our Father, Our King, primary phrase to prayers
Ba'al Teshuva:	A secular person who decided to become observant
Chassidim:	Followers of the Ba'al Shem Tov, leader of mystical movement in 18th century
Chazan:	Cantor
Chazanut:	Cantorial prayers in Synagogue
Chutzpa:	Impertinence
Glatt Kosher:	Strictly kosher
Haggada:	Booklet which is read on the first night of Pesach telling the story of the Exodus from Egypt
Halacha:	The body of Jewish Law
Hoshea:	Book of Hosea
Kabbala:	Jewish Mysticism
Korban Pesach:	Sacrifice to be brought in the Temple on the eve of Pesach. See *Shemot* 12: 1–28
Mashiach:	Messiah
Mezuzot:	Parchment scrolls affixed to the doorpost of rooms. See *Shemot* 12:7
Midrash:	Early rabbinic compendium of legal or narrative material
Minhag:	Jewish custom
Mishkan:	Tabernacle, Tent of Meeting
Mishna:	Early Rabbinic text of the Oral Law
Mishneh Torah:	Halachic codex by Maimonides
Mitzva:	Commandment or good deed
Moshe Rabbeinu:	Moses our teacher
Neshama:	Human soul
Olam Haba:	World to Come
Omer:	Official counting period of 49 days between Pesach and *Shavuot*. See *Vayikra* 23:15

Oral Torah:	Early authoritative rabbinic interpretation of the Five Books of Moses
Parasha:	Portion of the Torah read every Shabbat in the synagogue
Pirkei Avot:	Ethics of the Father, classic work on ethics, part of the Mishna
Pesach:	Passover, festival celebrating the Exodus from Egypt. See *Shemot* 34:25
Purim:	Festival of Esther as mentioned in the book of Esther
Rishonim:	Early Jewish Sages up until fifteenth century
Rosh Hashana:	Jewish New Year
Rosh HaYeshiva:	Dean of Talmudic college
Sanhedrin:	Ancient Supreme High Court of Israel or Tractate of the Talmud
Sephardim:	Jews who stayed for long periods in Spain, Portugal and other Mediterranean and Middle Eastern countries
Shabbat:	Seventh day of the week, rest day on which Jews are not allowed to work
Shavuot:	Pentacost, day of the giving of the Torah
Shir HaShirim:	Songs of Songs by King Solomon
Shmuel:	Book of Samuel
Shulchan Aruch:	Authoritative codex of Jewish Law written by Rabbi Yosef Karo
Sifri:	Early rabbinic Commentary to *Bamidbar* and *Devarim*
Talmud:	Largest compilation of Jewish writings of numerous volumes in which all of Jewish Law and Thought is represented in mainly dialogue form
Targumim:	Early rabbinic translations of Torah
Tefillin:	Phylacteries, two small leather black boxes containing scriptural passages which are bound by black leather strips on the left hand and on the head worn by Jewish men at the weekly morning prayers. See *Shemot* 13: 1–10
Tehillim:	Book of Psalms
Tzitzit:	Fringes attached to the four corners of a four-cornered garment reminding one of the commandments worn by men. See *Bamidbar* 15:37–41; *Shemot* 13:1–10

Sukkot:	Festival celebrating the journey of 40 years through the desert in which Jews sit in booths. See *Vayikra* 23:43
Torah:	Five books of Moses
Vayikra:	Book of Leviticus
Written Torah:	Pentateuch, Five books of Moses
Yechezkel:	Book of Ezekiel
Yeshaya:	Book of Isaiah
Yeshivot:	Talmudic Colleges
Yirmiyahu:	Book of Jeremiah
Yom Kippur:	Day of Atonement. Most important fast day on which one should repent. See *Vayikra* 16:29–31
Yom Tov:	Jewish festival

THOUGHTS IN WHICH JEWISH FESTIVALS
AND *PARASHAT HASHAVUA* APPEAR

BIOGRAPHICAL DETAILS OF FAMOUS
JEWISH THINKERS AND RABBIS
THROUGHOUT THE AGES
NOTED IN THIS WORK

Rabbi Eliezer Ashkenazi, 1513–86, Egypt, Europe, physician and Bible commentator

Rabbi Chaim Ibn Attar, Ohr HaChayim, 1696–1743, Morocco, Israel, kabbalist, talmudist and Bible commentator

Rabbi Naftali Zvi Yehuda Berlin, Netziv, 1817–93, last Rosh HaYeshiva of the famous Volozhin Yeshiva, Russia; talmudist and Bible commentator

Rabbi Shlomo Carlebach, 1926–1995, Germany, USA, Israel, composer of modern Jewish religious music

Rabbi Shmuel Eliezer Eidels, Maharsha, 1555–1631, Poland, foremost Talmud commentator

Rabbi Israel ben Eliezer, Ba'al Shem Tov, 1699–1760, Ukraine, founder and first leader of chassidism, thinker

Rabbi Yaacov Emden, 1697–1776, Germany, also known as *Yavetz*, halachic authority, kabbalist opposing the false messiah Shabbatai Zvi, one of the greatest scholars of his time

Rabbi Baruch HaLevi Epstein, 1860–1942, Russian talmudic scholar, Bible commentator

Avraham Ibn Ezra, 12th century, Toledo, Spain, Bible commentator, astronomer, poet, grammarian

Rabbi Yerachmiel David Fried, Jerusalem; Texas, contemporary halachic authority, author

Rabbi Hai Gaon, one of the greatest halachic authorities of the 10th century, Pumbedita, Babylon

Rabbi Meir Simcha HaCohen, 1843–1926, Dvinsk, Talmudist, and Bible commentator

Rabbi Samson Raphael Hirsch, 1808–88, Frankfurt, Germany, founder of Modern Orthodoxy, author and Bible commentator

Rabbi Yitschak Hutner, 1907–1980, head of American Yeshiva, thinker

Rabbi Moshe Isserles, Rema, 1530–1572, Krakow, one of the greatest halachic authorities, author of many works and most important codifier

Rabbi Yaakov Kamenetsky, 1891–1986, Tiktin, Lithuania; Seattle, WA, Monsey, NY; Toronto, Ontario, leader of American Orthodoxy, author and Bible commentator

Rabbi Yeshaya Karelitz, Chazon Ish, 1878–1953, one of the greatest halachic authorities, author and thinker

Rabbi Yosef Karo, 15–16th century, author of *Shulchan Aruch*, a most important halachic compendium of Jewish Law, kabbalist

Rabbi David Kimchi, Radak, 1160–1236, Provence, Bible commentator

Rabbi Eliyahu Kitov, 20th century, Israeli author

Rav Avraham Yitschak Kook, 1865–1935, Chief Rabbi of Palestine and Israel, halachic authority, kabbalist, most influential thinker and religious Zionist leader

Yeshayahu Leibowitz, 1904–94, Russia, Israel, professor of science in Hebrew University, Jerusalem, philosopher and Bible commentator

Rabbi Yerucham Levovitz, 20th century, head of the Yeshiva of Mir in Poland

Maharal of Prague, 1525–1609, famous kabbalist and thinker

Rabbi Yaakov Tzevi Mecklenburg, 1785–1865, Poland, Bible commentator

Rabbi Shmuel Mohilewer, 1824–98, rabbi of Bialystock, Poland, founder of religious Zionism

Rabbi Moshe ben Nachman, Ramban, (Nachmanides), 1194–1270, Spain, Israel, one of the greatest Bible commentators

Rambam, Maimonides, 1135–1204, Spain, Egypt and Israel, greatest Jewish philosopher and codifier of Jewish Law

Rabbi Menachem Recanati, one of the great kabbalists of the 13th–14th century, Italy

Franz Rosenzweig, 1886–1929, Germany, thinker and author, co-translator of the Bible in German

Rabbi Ovadia Sforno, 1475–1550, Italy, Bible commentator and physician

Rabbi Joseph B. Soloveitchik, 1903–1993, Boston, leader of Modern Orthodoxy in the USA, talmudist, halachic authority and influential thinker

Rabbi Moshe Sofer, Chatam Sofer, 1762–1839, Germany, Hungary, halachic authority, leader of Hungarian Jewry, Bible commentator

Da'at Ba'alei Tosafot, 13th century, France, a compendium of Torah commentary, originating with the Tosafists

Rabbi Yechiel Weinberg, 1885–1966, halachic authority and scholar, head of the Berlin Rabbinical Seminar

Rabbi Yaakov David Wilowsky, Ridbaz, 1845–1913, Lithuanian talmudist, halachic authority

Rabbi Yechiel of Paris, 13th century, French Talmudist and Tosafist, leading Jewish protagonist in "the disputation of Paris" held at the court of Louis IX, died in Israel.

Rabbi Shlomo Yitzchaki, Rashi, 1040–1105, most famous Bible commentator

BIOGRAPHICAL DETAILS OF WESTERN THINKERS NOTED IN THIS WORK

Thomas Aquinas, 1225–74, Italy, Catholic thinker, creator of "Thomistic" philosophy

Aristotle, 384–22 BCE, Greece, philosopher, student of Plato, teacher of Alexander the Great, "Father of Logic"

Ibn Rosh Averroes, 1126–98, Spain, Arab philosopher

Johann Sebastian Bach, 1685–1750, Germany, composer

Emile Benveniste, 1902–76, France, author

Godfried J. A. Bomans, 1913–71, Holland, Haarlem, Dutch author

G. K. Chesterton, 1874–1936, England, English author

Frank Moore Colby, 1865–1925, USA, author

Uriel De Costa, 1585–1630, Sephardi Dutch author, several times excommunicated by the Amsterdam Sephardi community

Charles Robert Darwin, 1809–82, Shrewsbury-Down, England, father of the Theory of Evolution

Alan M. Dershowitz, 1938–, New York, Boston, Harvard Law Professor

Friedrich Durrenmatt, 1921–90, Switzerland, Swiss playwright

Shraga Fisherman, 1958–, Israel, Israeli author and researcher

David Flusser, 1917–2000, Germany, Jerusalem, professor of New Testament Studies, Hebrew University

John Fowles, 1926–, England, English author

Sigmund Freud, 1856–1939, Vienna, London, father of psychoanalysis

Erich Fromm, 1900–80, Frankfurt, New York, psychoanalyst

Johann Wolfgang Goethe, 1749–1832, Germany, greatest German poet

Rene Goscinny, 1926–77 and Albert Uderzo, 1927–, France, cartoonists

Georg Wilhelm Friedrich Hegel, 1770–1831, Germany, philosopher, most influential on modern philosophy

Carl Gustaf Jung, 1875–1961, Basle-Zurich, father of modern psychology

Emanuel Kant, 1724–1804, Germany, famous philosopher

Frank Leahy, 1908–73, Indiana, football coach

Richard Livingstone, 1880–1960, England, author

John Locke, 1632–1704, England, philosopher and psychologist, father of empiricism

Jacques Maritain, 1882–1973, France, French author and thinker

Ogden Nash, 1902–71, USA, poet

John Henry Newman, 1801–90, England, cardinal, originally of the Anglican Church

Friedrich Nietzsche, 1844–1900, Germany, philosopher

Naso Ovidius, 43 BCE–17 AD, Rome, poet of great influence

Isaac Bashevis Singer, 1904–91, Poland, New York, Yiddish-English novelist, Nobel Prize Winner 1978

Logan Pearsall Smith, 1865–1946, USA, England, author

Plato, 427–347 BCE, Greece, student of Socrates, teacher of Aristotle, major figure in Greek philosophy

William Robertson Smith, Keig, 1846–94, Cambridge, Orientalist

Arthur Schopenhauer, 1788–1860, Leipzig, Frankfurt, German philosopher

George Bernard Shaw, 1854–1945, England, author

Benedictus (Baruch) Spinoza, 1632–77, Amsterdam, Dutch philosopher and Jewish apostate

Arnold J. Toynbee, 1889–1975, England, historian

Mark Twain, 1835–1910, USA, an influential author

Herbert George Wells, England 1866–1946, author

Ludwig Josef Johann Wittgenstein, 1889–1951, England, philosopher